Praise for Barb Rogers ar

"*Keep It Simple & Sane* is a simple, heartfelt, refreshingly honest look at how to keep life simple and meaningful. A book that will benefit everyone who reads it."

—ELIZABETH ENGSTROM, author of *The Northwoods Chronicles*

"Barb Rogers offers help, peace, and encouragement to those ready to change their lives for the good."

—THOMAS BIEN, PH.D., author of *Mindful Recovery: A Spiritual Path to Healing from Addiction*

"Extremely helpful for anyone who is trying to find a way to deal with 'stinking thinking' and establish a healthier balance in life. *Keep It Simple & Sane* definitely deserves a spot your bookshelf."

—ALLEN BERGER, PH.D., psychologist and author of *12 Stupid Things That Mess Up Recovery*

"Barb Rogers weaves her tragic story of addiction and miraculous recovery within the tapestry of thoughtful and sensible suggestions for discovering and maintaining a lifetime of peace. She is a wonderful example of what *the promises* tell us await us."

—KAREN CASEY, PH.D., author of *Codependence and the Power of Detachment*

12 steps
that can save
your life

Real-Life Stories
from People Who Are
Walking the Walk

12 steps
that can save
your life

Barb Rogers

Conari Press

Turner Publishing Company
Nashville, Tennessee
www.turnerpublishing.com

ISBN: 978-1-57324-422-0
LIBRARY OF CONGRESS CATALOGING-IN-PUBLICATION DATA
Rogers, Barb, 1947–
   12 steps that can save your life : real-life stories from people who are walking the
walk / Barb Rogers.
       p. cm.
       ISBN 978-1-57324-422-0 (alk. paper)
   1. Substance abuse—Treatment. 2. Addicts—Rehabilitation. 3. Twelve-step programs. I. Title. II. Title: Twelve steps that can save your life.
   HV4998.R64 2009
   616.86'060922—dc22   2009005690

Cover and text design by Maxine Ressler
Typeset in Bembo Std, Impressum, and NeutraText Cover
photograph © iStockphoto.com/Agnes Csondor

Printed in the United States of America

10   9   8   7   6   5   4   3   2

Contents

Introduction

George P., an auto mechanic from Illinois, says, "I am an alcoholic. I will be an alcoholic until the day I die. And if I don't keep something between me and the bottle, I *will* drink again." George's addiction is alcohol, but that statement can apply to any addiction. It is simply human nature to attempt to fill a hole left in us by one thing with something else. Otherwise, we run the danger of returning to what was familiar.

Imagine that you have been living in the same space for years. All your furniture is in place, right where you want it. It's a comfortable place. Suddenly, your couch disappears. From that moment on, every time you walk into that room your attention is drawn to the empty space previously occupied by the couch. Until you find something to replace it, there will be a feeling of something missing in your life. Isn't that where addiction begins?

In my more than twenty-five years in recovery from my own addictions, listening to the stories of others, I've discovered some common threads that weave us together no matter the addiction. The most common thread is that something is missing. Like the couch, it's the only thing on which we can focus. We find something to fill the hole in our lives. It works for a while, and then it becomes an addiction that takes over our lives. It never works for long, because we can't replace a couch with a table. A couch and a table serve two entirely different purposes.

What is missing in your life? Is it love, acceptance, self-esteem, self-respect, the respect of others, unfulfilled expectations of what you imagined your life should be, or perhaps control? What are you using to replace the missing part of you? Does it work? You will know whether something is working because you will know what it is to live a contented, happy life. How's it going? Are you content, or confused? Are you happy, or frustrated? Are you at peace, or full of fear? Do you look forward to the day ahead, or do you dread it?

12 Steps: Cult, Curse, or Cure?

Many thoughts, ideas, concepts, and even studies have been focused on overcoming addiction, but by far the most widely used and most successful solution for over seventy years has been a 12-step program that originated with Bill W. and Dr. Bob, for those suffering from alcoholism. What is it about the 12-step program, used today for every imaginable addiction, that has successfully changed the lives of those seemingly helpless, hopeless addicts?

Is it a cult? To qualify as a cult, a movement must have a leader, or an overreaching concept, by which everyone involved is ruled. There is no guru, president, board, or religious leader running any 12-step program. Every participant is as important as the next and is entitled to her own beliefs and opinions. There are no rules—only twelve "suggested" steps. It is entirely up to each individual if, when, and how he chooses to incorporate any, or all, of the steps into his life. What's the cost? There are no fees, initiations, hazing, or rejection. If a person believes she belongs in a meeting, she does, and if she's strapped, with no money to put into the basket, it doesn't matter. The only requirement is a desire to find a better way of life, free of addiction. It doesn't even have to be an honest desire.

Is it a curse? Many who return to a 12-step meeting after a relapse say, "There's nothing worse than a belly full of booze and a head full of AA" (referring to the original 12-step program, Alcoholics Anonymous). Once they have discovered a solution, those who continue on with their addiction, whatever it might be, know the curse of conflict. Through the period of addiction, the addict may convince himself there's no way out, but once the addict has been introduced to a 12-step meeting, and to others who have overcome the same addiction and come out on the other side, there is no more justification for continuing in the addiction.

Some—particularly those around the addict—may consider a 12-step program as a curse. During the process of working the steps, the addict will go through many profound changes. For those who have been active participants, codependents, or caretakers, the changes may not be welcome: There is comfort in predictability. Therefore, what happens when the recovering addict begins to think differently—to act, and react, in an unpredictable way?

Active participants may attempt to lure the person back into addiction. It's not that they don't care about the person as much as they can; it's that, above all things, they must protect their rationalization to continue in their own addiction. They will say things like:

"You could have just one drink. One won't hurt you."

"Have you put on weight?"

"It's just a penny game of cards. Surely that won't hurt you."

"You can go back on your diet tomorrow."

"Your house doesn't look that bad. You can clean it later."

"If you pay your car payment late, you can buy this. It's on sale now, and you really need it."

"A little pot won't hurt you."

"It was prescribed by a doctor. He wouldn't give you something addictive."

The codependent might feel perturbed because she tells herself she's been trying to help for years and now the addict is listening to complete strangers, people who can't possibly care as much as she. The truth is that codependents feel as if they are losing something—control over an active addict, an excuse to continue their own questionable behavior, the ability to martyr themselves before the world. There will simply be no more statements like "Poor Mary. She's put up with so much for so long" or "Jim must be a saint. I don't know how he deals with her." Addicts who choose recovery make a decision, and codependents are thrust into that decision.

A caretaker, or enabler, tells himself he is protecting the addict. That's his job, or role, in life. It gives him purpose. Take away that purpose, and you invite fear and panic. As long as the addict is active, the caretaker is needed. Feelings of panic are caused by the fear of no longer being important or needed in the recovering addict's life. These feelings can give rise to statements such as "Those people are brainwashing you. We can handle this together. I know what you need"; "Those people are more important to you than I am. You don't really have to go to a meeting tonight, do you?"; and "You aren't that bad. All we need is a vacation, to get away from everything for a while."

The curse of a 12-step program of recovery is in the eye of the beholder—what he or she has to gain or lose, real or imagined. For the addict, who is dealing with a constant compulsion to repeat self-destructive behaviors, it's all about hope.

Your stomach is churning. A watery feeling is gurgling in the back of your throat. You know it's coming: you're going to throw up. You don't want to make a mess, humiliate yourself, embarrass others—but there's no stopping it. If you try to use willpower in that moment, you will have a bit of understanding of what it feels like to be addicted. Addiction hides like a dormant seed in frozen soil. Once nurtured, it takes root to burst forth yet again, spreading even more seeds far and wide. What would it be like to find every seed, dig it up, and destroy it? The solution, then, is to keep the seeds dormant. That is the goal of a 12-step program. It teaches awareness that the seed of addiction is there, and that there is a way to keep it dormant but no promise of a cure.

To cure a problem is to eliminate it entirely. In my experience, once the line is crossed into addiction, there is no going back. There are those who would disagree with that premise, who would say that with proper medication, therapy, and other methods the addict can be returned to a normal state. I, and others like me, grabbed on to that idea like a lifeline, and it nearly killed us. The seed was still there, waiting patiently for its moment in the sun to take root, to thrive again.

Whether it's a mental obsession, an emotional compulsion, or a physical addiction, it can bring the addict to a state of mental, physical, and spiritual bankruptcy. Therefore, the person must be treated for all these conditions. Therein lies the beauty of a 12-step program. Only the first step gives a name to the addiction. The following eleven steps are a guide that allows the addict, on his own terms, to discover the causes and effects of the addiction and offers him a way to keep the seeds of addiction dormant.

The Twelve Steps are neither a cult, a curse, nor a cure for addicts. They are simply a set of suggestions, based on the experience of former addicts, that have worked. Using the steps as tools, those people found a way to be happy, joyous, and free. The idea is: if you want what we have, do what we did, and it will be possible. It is a statement of hope.

Bottom's Up

People don't wake up one morning and think it would be fun if they attended a 12-step meeting or checked into a treatment facility. That particular decision must be preceded by hitting bottom. Hitting bottom is as individual as each human being. The one common denominator is that it is a particular moment when the addict runs headlong into the reality of his or her situation, admits the truth, and seeks a way out.

Cemeteries are full of those who, like my mother, decided that there was only one way out—and took their own lives. Some, like my friends David W., Frank P., and Lynda T., mistakenly believed there would always be time and then, in the end, found that they could not reverse the ravages of their addictions. Others cross that fine line into insanity and spend their lives medicated and in and out of mental institutions. Prisons house those whose addiction brought them to a desperate moment in which the addiction, and not they themselves, made a poor choice.

Then there are the lucky ones: those who hit bottom, find help, and discover a way out of that seemingly bottomless pit of addiction.

Whatever the addiction, it takes what it takes for the person suffering from it to hit bottom. There are "soft" bottoms and "hard" bottoms. Many years ago, I met Millie. She shared her story with me. Well into her seventies and looking like someone's rotund, gray-haired granny, Millie had been in a 12-step program for years, or so I assumed. Not so. I was amazed when she told me she'd been in recovery from alcoholism for only a few months. Millie and her husband had been married for many years, raised their children, owned an enormous dairy farm, and had done quite well in life. Suddenly, her husband died from a heart attack. Millie was left to run the business. It was more difficult than she imagined, requiring long hours and mounds of paperwork. She remembered that her husband would have a few drinks at the end of the day while working on bills and invoices. And so, though she'd never had a drink of alcohol in her life, she decided to try it.

Millie said to me, "I must have been an alcoholic waiting to add alcohol." Within three years, Millie couldn't stop drinking. Her children and grandchildren did an intervention. That was her bottom. She hit a "soft" bottom: she didn't lose her business, family, or money. Later, she married an older man she met at a meeting, and they lived a wonderful life together until they both passed away.

On the other hand, there is the story I heard from Willie D. He worked hard, advancing to a position of importance in a big company. He achieved the American dream: a big house, two new cars in the garage, a beautiful wife, children, and enough money to have pretty much what he and his family desired. When gambling was legalized where he lived, curiosity lured him to a new casino. At first he'd stop in at the casino on his way home from work, just for an hour or so, and give himself a financial limit. One evening he hit it big, and from that moment on he was hooked.

His wife began to resent the time he spent away from her, so Willie brought her along. She felt the thrill of gambling, the escape from her everyday life. Little by little, the money drained away; they were unable to pay the mortgage or the utilities, make the car payments, or keep their children in private schools. His wife panicked; she took the children and left. Willie, desperate for money, and telling himself that if he could just hit it big one more time he would pay off the bills that were piling up, embezzled from his company. He had every intention of paying off the bills and returning the money as quickly as possible, but he found himself back at the casino.

The bank took Willie's house, the car dealers repossessed the cars, and he had no idea as to the whereabouts of his wife and children. He could no longer face family and friends, many of whom he owed money to. The only thing he'd held on to was his job, and he knew it would be only a short time before the company discovered what he'd done. He would go to prison. Alone, in a filthy rented room, with a bottle of whiskey and his wife's sleeping pills, he contemplated his death.

As thoughts whirled through his mind, he recalled a flier about Gamblers Anonymous posted in the men's room at the casino. He walked to the casino, past the gambling tables and machines to the bathroom, wrote down the phone number, and made the call. He'd hit a "hard" bottom, and for him that was what it took to admit the problem and seek help.

When I met Willie, he was celebrating ten years without gambling. He'd gone to his boss, owned up to the embezzling, lost his job, and worked out a plan for repayment. It would take a long time, but at least they didn't prosecute. He began working for a tax business and then started his own business, which was thriving. I don't know what happened with his wife and kids. There are some things we can never get back. I hope he found his way back to them, at least to make amends. If he couldn't make amends to them, he was making the amends he could by continuing to attend meetings and helping others who suffered from the same addiction.

The particulars of hitting a bottom can be unique, but no matter the addiction, the feelings are the same: feelings of hopelessness, and helplessness, over an addiction that has taken control of one's life. The necessity of hitting bottom applies to all addictions, because it is in that moment that the addict becomes willing to do whatever it takes to change. Hitting bottom is the catalyst, and becoming willing is the beginning.

Just as all addictions are based in fear, so is the concept of recovery. I recently heard Pat, a woman visiting our local meeting from Oregon, say that fear can be interpreted in one of two ways.

Forget Everything and Run

or

Face Everything and Recover

She nailed it! That is the choice we make when we hit bottom. So, we walk into our first meeting, or check into a treatment center, and are faced with twelve pretty daunting steps. Will they make us uncomfortable? Absolutely. They are set up to make us uncomfortable. God knows, I spent my life making everyone around me as uncomfortable as possible.

The first encounter with the steps sends addicts' minds into fear-based mental gymnastics. I remember some of mine:

What have I done?

What have I gotten myself into?

Who would do those things [the steps]?

I can't do all that stuff. I won't do all that stuff.

If I'd wanted to talk to God, I'd have gone to church.

I tried that. It didn't work.

I'm not telling anyone all my stuff.

This is crazy. No one really does all that stuff, do they?

I've got to get out of here.

However, it was too late. I had to sit through the meeting. Amazingly, I heard exactly what I needed to hear. One man said, "You have your whole life to work this program. You don't have to do it all today." Another said, "The steps are not rules, but are suggestions for those who want recovery from addiction." One rather gruff-looking individual said, "From this day forward, you have a choice, and you never have to be alone again."

That last statement caused a swell of emotions inside me, and brought tears to my eyes. Unable to deal with the emotions, afraid they would send me over the edge yet again, I left the meeting, indulged in my addictions, and tried to blot out the words haunting my mind. I was exhausted: tired of getting up every day; of facing myself, others, the world around me; of always feeling sick and tired, disappointed, and disgusted . . . and so alone. I returned to the meeting. I'd truly hit bottom.

Uncomfortable? I'd lived in the world of addiction so long, held on to my excuses and pain (much of which was self-induced) so hard, that anything outside of the life I'd known was uncomfortable. I will never forget the moment when Jack C. said, "Uncomfortable is a gift. Change is uncomfortable. But isn't that why you're here?" Like I said before, we don't simply decide it might be interesting to go to a 12-step meeting or check into treatment. We go because we are desperate for change. The choice is always preceded by hitting bottom, no matter how "soft" or "hard" that bottom is. It takes exactly what it takes for each addict to hit his personal bottom.

Steppin'

Recently, I heard Gina G., a twenty-five-year-old woman suffering from several addictions, say, "I'm steppin'. I've been steppin', one way or another, all of my life. It's just a new set of steps." I'd been working the Twelve Steps for as long as she'd been alive, but I'd never heard it put so simply, or so profoundly. All of life is about the steps of progression.

With each new step you take, whether it's from crawling to standing or from walking to driving an automobile, there will be new experiences and people, and a change of perception of the world in which you live. Problems happen when you get stuck, and addictions are about getting stuck.

For those who have crossed the line into an addiction, it's like living the same day over and over, with others and situations filtered through the addiction. Gina lived in a long-term treatment facility, where she'd accumulated three months free of her addictions. As she continued her story, I listened intently. She grew up in California, the only child of a determined stage mother who had grand designs and expectations for her. She would be a "star."

Gina learned to dance, one step at a time; to sing, one note at a time; to play piano; to walk, talk, and look in just the right way—all to please others. Although she never accomplished much as an actress, except in crowd scenes, she did well in modeling. That's where she crossed the line and got stuck. Her secret life began. She had to carefully seek out places to purge, stayed up after everyone went to sleep to exercise, and became addicted to enemas and diet pills. Every day, every action, every thought revolved around her addictions and keeping hidden the horrible secrets that were destroying her life. She said, "I got so thin, I looked like a hanger, but it was never enough. I couldn't let anyone close to me for fear they would discover the truth."

All addictions are about secrets, lies, manipulations, fear, and loneliness. However, there is good news. In a way, the steps of recovery set forth in a 12-step program are like going through a rebirthing. You get to start over and learn a new way, step by step, to get unstuck. Like every learning process in life, you must begin by becoming willing, then taking the first step. Willingness happens when you hit your personal bottom. The first step deals with your acknowledging the addiction that is controlling your life—how it is affecting you and the way you live.

Join me, and the stories of others, on this journey to recovery through the Twelve Steps—how they work, and why they work. You have nothing to lose, and a life beyond your wildest dreams to gain. Let's go steppin'.

The Twelve Steps

1. We admitted we were powerless over our addiction, that our lives had become unmanageable.

2. Came to believe that a power greater than ourselves could restore us to sanity.

3. Made a decision to turn our will and our lives over to the care of God as we understood God.

4. Made a searching and fearless moral inventory of ourselves.

5. Admitted to God, to ourselves, and to another human being the exact nature of our wrongs.

6. Were entirely ready to have God remove all these defects of character.

7. Humbly asked God to remove our shortcomings.

8. Made a list of all persons we had harmed, and became willing to make amends to them all.

9. Made direct amends to such people wherever possible, except when to do so would injure them or others.

10. Continued to take personal inventory and when we were wrong promptly admitted it.

11. Sought through prayer and meditation to improve our conscious contact with God as we understand God, praying only for knowledge of God's will for us and the power to carry that out.

12. Having had a spiritual awakening as the result of these steps, we tried to carry this message to addicts, and to practice these principles in all our affairs.

—adapted from *Alcoholics Anonymous*

Part I

the
action steps

Step 1

We admitted we were powerless over our addiction, that our lives had become unmanageable.

In recent years, as I was attending meetings and working with other addicts, a new trend became apparent to me. Many who are seeking recovery suffer from more than one addiction. Others, in recovery from one addiction, grab on to another. I believe the situation has been there all along but has only recently made its way to the forefront. The reason is that to be free of addiction, the addict must be free of all addictions and aware of the impulse to substitute addictions.

When you think of it, it makes sense. Alcoholics don't handle drugs or sex any better than they do booze. Take away an overeater's food and he may find his comfort, or escape, in a liquid diet, pills, sex, shopping, or a wall of clutter. Many recovering drug addicts believe they can drink. I have yet to meet one who has accomplished this success-fully. For addicts, a drug is a drug, wet or dry.

Mary S., who attended Overeaters Anonymous for years, ended up in an AA meeting. She said, "After my gastric bypass, I was on a liquid diet. No one told me that didn't involve gin. As a drunk, I convinced myself it would be OK to eat those things I knew I shouldn't eat when I was sober. I damn near killed myself."

For thirteen years I've watched Nancy D., who started out in recovery from alcohol and sex, move on to an addiction to prescription drugs, gambling, and now overeating. You would be amazed at how many addicts are sitting in 12-step meetings addicted to prescription drugs. I am not a doctor, but my personal experience, and what others have confided in me, has convinced me that it is nearly impossible to get a clear diagnosis of a mental disorder until the addiction is addressed. Therefore, many of the prescribed drugs simply mask the problem and become a secondary addiction.

It's a chicken-and-egg thing. Was Nancy indulging in addictions because she suffered from clinical depression, or did the feelings of a lack of control, helplessness, and hope-lessness caused by her addictions bring on the depression?

After a lengthy stay in a mental hospital, where I was diagnosed with post-traumatic stress disorder, manic depression, borderline schizophrenia, and God only knows what else, they released me with a bag of colorful pills. I would be taking up to eleven pills a day. There were pills to keep me up, put me down, level me out, and keep me from thinking. It didn't take me long to figure out I didn't want to live without the ability to put two thoughts together in a rational way. That, coupled with my fear of prescription drugs—I had watched my addicted mother take her own life at age thirty-nine—brought me to the toilet, where I flushed all the pills.

Anyone who has been addicted or has dealt with addicts will understand how a doctor might misdiagnose an addict. The other personality that emerges when an alcoholic drinks could be seen as a symptom of schizophrenia. The extreme high that a drinker, a drug addict, a gambler, an overeater, a sex addict, an anorexic, or a shopper feels when he is flush with product or any other sought-after feeling is counteracted by the extreme low when the opposite is true. It looks like manic depression. Addicts do not fall into addiction without a reason. They are brought to addiction through that unnamed "something" that has caused a hole in their lives that they are trying to fill. Post-traumatic stress disorder?

There are real chemical imbalances that can cause mental problems and will be solved with the right medications. However, with an addict, how can one tell where the addiction ends and the mental problem begins without first acknowledging the addiction and dealing with it? Medication may seem like the easier, softer way, but in the long run all it does, if there is no real chemical imbalance, is enable the addict to continue down a self-destructive, unhappy path.

I did not suffer from all those mental problems I was diagnosed with and for which I was medicated. I suffered from addictions, and until I was willing to look at them and find a way to get help, my life would only get worse. Which brings me to step 1 of a 12-step program. It is absolutely the most important of the Twelve Steps. Without working it honestly and completely, you will have no healthy way to continue. This step is stated in two sections: (1) admitting the nature of the addiction we are powerless over; and (2) recognizing how it is affecting our lives.

Taking step 1 is like hitting a wall of truth. It is not easy for addicts to accept the truth. If they do, the words are spoken aloud, the cat is out of the bag, and they will feel compelled to do something about it. However, like any other disease, until the suffering individual faces it head-on and accepts it as a reality, solutions will escape her. There is no solution for something that is not perceived as a problem.

What the problem is, is addressed in the second part of the first step: how is your particular addiction affecting your life? Is it taking you to places you don't want to go? Are you doing things you wouldn't normally consider? Is it affecting your health, mentally, emotionally, or physically, in a negative way? Is it affecting your relationships at home, or maybe at work? Are you pushing away those people who care enough about you to tell you the truth? When you consider what you have given up for your addiction, it doesn't necessarily involve things. It can be time, contentment, happiness, self-respect, or any number of other things. The second half of the step is a revelation of loss.

Donna G. was a cheerleader, majorette, and prom queen in high school—beautiful, intelligent, and popular. She was the epitome of what young women attempt to achieve. She knew exactly what was expected of her and discovered early in life that appearances meant everything. To the outsider, her life seemed ideal. But Donna lived with a big secret.

Through the week, she played her part well, running with the "in" crowd, making good grades, and she was well thought of. When the weekends and school vacations rolled around, though, she disappeared into oblivion with a whole other crowd of friends, who lived to party.

As I listened to her story, I could picture her at home, stressed over her parents' failing marriage, trying to keep up appearances outside the home, until one day when she went into the bathroom to wash her hair. Someone told her that if she rinsed her hair with beer, it would make it shiny. It took very little beer to wash her hair, so she drank the rest. A feeling only another addict can truly understand came over her. It was the beginning of a downward spiral that would culminate many years later in her facing step 1 in a 12-step meeting.

Donna went away to college, a real party school, and flunked out the second semester. She became a stewardess for a major airline in New York but got fired for stealing miniature bottles, and finally married a man she barely knew, believing that to be a solution to her problems. In a very short time, after one of her drunken escapades that ended with her in a hospital while her husband was out of town, she knew her marriage was failing. She went to a 12-step meeting. It took only one meeting to convince her she was not like "those" people. Yes, she might have a little drinking problem, but her life was not unmanageable.

Donna had not lost enough to admit the unmanage-ability of her life caused by an addiction to alcohol. Rather than face that first step, Donna spent years in and out of hospitals and detox centers. She tried everything: she attended and worked in her church, even went to the occasional AA meeting. But she couldn't accept that the first step applied to her. There had to be a way to figure it out. After all, she was an intelligent woman. She told me, "I realized my choice was to live without alcohol and exist in constant emotional torture, or continue drinking and deal with physical suffer-ing and mental torture. It never occurred to me there was another choice."

She hit her bottom in a motel room in Flagstaff, Ari-zona, with little memory of how that happened. The last thing she recalled was being bailed out of jail by her priest, who was also her boss; him driving her away from the jail; and him putting her out on the side of the road, where he informed her he was giving her to God. With the realization of how unmanageable her life was, of all that she'd given up to indulge her addiction, she fell to her knees in that motel room and said, "God, whatever it is that helps those people in AA, please let it help me." Donna had taken the first step honestly and completely. From that moment on, she would be able to move forward to a new way of life.

You see, taking step 1 doesn't have to happen in a meeting. It has to happen within you; the deepest part of you has to become willing to admit the truth. If you are looking for a solution in a 12-step program, no matter the addiction you suffer from, it will require that one moment when you can no longer lie to yourself or rationalize or justify your actions. It is when you stand naked in front of yourself and become willing to do whatever it takes to change.

Just as there was a beginning to your addiction, there is a beginning to recovery. That beginning is step 1.

Step 2

We came to believe that a power greater than ourselves could restore us to sanity.

Those who are sane, who live in a healthy state of mind, learn not only from personal experience but also from the experience of others. This is not true for those suffering from addictions. They continue the same behavior over and over, expecting different results. Before Neva G. passed away, one of her favorite sayings in meetings was "If every time you ate chili it made you sick, wouldn't you stop eating chili? A sane person would." That sums up the insanity of addiction.

Addicts live in a small, controlled world. They avoid others who don't "understand" them. Dick B., a married man with a few years in recovery from alcoholism, sat in his garage, a drink in his hand, tears running down his face, and shared with me what took him back to drinking. Little by little, I discovered the truth. It seemed that he had been sneaking alcohol for some time, but things came to a head when his wife informed him they would be taking a trip that would require days of driving, overnights in motels, and staying with relatives. He panicked and checked himself into a seventy-two-hour detox center that night. I assumed he felt that three days in detox, where he was kept drugged, were preferable to a two-week trip where he couldn't get away from wife, and others, to indulge his addiction.

Do you think it is any different for the gambler, the compulsive eater, the sex addict, the anorexic, the drug addict—even those who suffer from those seemingly healthier addictions like exercise and compulsive cleanliness? Some of the stories that have convinced me this is true are the following:

Ben T. would fill the window-washer-fluid bottle of his car with booze and every so many miles would say to his wife, "Do you hear that? I think I better check under the hood." He'd pull the car over to the side of the road, open the hood, pull a straw out of his pocket, and have a drink. It was the only way he could get through a trip.

Mary S., an anorexic from California, invented ways to move food around on her plate so it appeared she was eating; she would store food in her cheeks and transfer it to a napkin or into the toilet if she was not in a place where she could purge. Late into the night, when the house was still, she'd sneak into the walk-in closet and exercise furiously.

Lonnie S. lied to the woman with whom he lived and whom he planned to marry, telling her he was mugged on the way to the bank to deposit cash to pay bills. He even went along when she called the police, and repeated his lie to them. She didn't find out until too late that he hadn't made the car payment or paid the insurance or the rent for a while. He told her he was going off to speak to other suffering gamblers or to attend a meeting when in fact he was getting away from the house to gamble. He eventually lost everything, including the woman he swore was the love of his life.

Donna R., whose surroundings had to be perfect, got to a point of hardly being able to leave her house. She felt safe there with everything spotless and in its place. Absolutely nothing, and no one, including her husband and children, could live up to her standards. While she told herself they were driving her crazy with their messy ways, she was driving them away. She refused to eat out in "filthy" restaurants, but all restaurants were filthy in her mind. She could bear to stay in someone else's house or a motel only if she brought her own disinfected bedding and cleaning supplies. Even then, if there was something she couldn't fix, change, or get clean enough, it wasn't going to happen. You can only imagine what her vacations were like.

Jane D., a young female addict, told me the story of her insanity. Money was in short supply; she'd just started a new job and would not have a paycheck for two weeks.

She barely had enough money to buy the drugs to get her through. After she bought her drugs, afraid she would use them all up too quickly, she went to her girlfriend down the hall and asked if she could leave half of the drugs with her. She told her friend not to give them back until a certain date no matter how much she begged for them. Sure enough, she ran out sooner than expected. Desperate, she broke into her friend's apartment, ransacked it looking for them, and was arrested for stealing her own drugs.

These stories are but a small sampling of how addicts hold on to the insanity of addiction. The things they do while in the throes of addiction are not who they really are, or who they want to be. Many will try a myriad of ways to stop, but in a short time, they find themselves right back where they started. They have lost the power to control the situation, or the substance.

Let's talk about power. If you made a list right now of the five most powerful people you know of, who would they be? Go ahead, write them down. Next to each name, write down why you see that person as powerful. If you chose people who are politically influential, have great wealth, or are famous, you might be surprised what you would see if you could be a fly on the wall in their day-to-day lives. True power is the ability to act and to produce an effect. People who can do that in a positive way each day, no matter what life throws at them, are powerful.

I am fortunate indeed to have been put in a position in life of overcoming seemingly insurmountable odds and watching others do the same. There are many of us who to the outside world looked like hopeless cases, who contributed nothing to others and the world around us. If you asked us what changed, we would tell you that the first thing we did was open our minds to the possibility of a Higher Power.

It's not easy for many in recovery to wrap their minds around that possibility. Many of us have had lives filled with trauma, fear, frustration, and rage, and many times we placed the blame on a God we weren't even sure was there. Others were abused and frightened in a religious setting.

At age seventeen, as I stood in the hospital, my little girl dead in my arms, my in-laws' preacher said to me, "God needed a little angel." I can't repeat in print what I said to him. Why would this man's God take my daughter, who had fought so hard to live? At age nineteen I lived through nearly the same scenario with my youngest son, followed closely by my mother's suicide. God! God? They had to be crazy. Why would I want anything to do with a God? I didn't have much, but he took it all away. Later, when I lost another child before birth, and my fifteen-year-old son, who was the light of my life and the last child I would ever have, was killed, all I wanted was to be released from the pain that had settled inside me like a tangible thing. I used one addiction after another in an attempt to ease the pain, but it lived on.

Tom B., brought up in a strict religious household and forced to attend a religious school for twelve years, said,

"The God I learned about scared me. He was just sitting up there waiting to punish me when I didn't live up to his expectations, and I didn't know how anyone could do that. Finally, I stopped trying."

Tom said, "When the guy from a 12-step meeting mentioned a Higher Power, which to me meant God, all those old thoughts reemerged. If I hadn't been so desperate, in a hopeless state of body and mind, I would have run away. But the only other options I was facing were insanity or death."

The man from the 12-step meeting shared with Tom what it meant to believe in a power greater than himself— that it would be a God of his understanding that had nothing to do with what he'd learned as a child. It took a while, but Tom attended the meetings, listened to the experiences of others, and began to wonder if what they'd done might work for him. He discovered he was not a bad person, but a person who did bad things in the throes of his addiction and because of his feelings of hopelessness and desperation; he decided he might become willing to try again.

Tom and I may have reached that moment of desperation through different circumstances, but we shared the same feelings and were both faced with a choice. We could return to what we had been doing, which made our lives a daily exercise in misery, or open our minds to the possibility of a Higher Power that could do for us what we had not been able to do for ourselves. It would be a choice that would forever change our lives.

If you met Tom today, you would see a loving husband, a devoted father, a true friend—compassionate, loving, and kind. He has become the man in the other chair, who now shares his experience, strength, and hope with others in their moment of desperation. I've heard him say, "For me, sanity is knowing I can't do this on my own, and I don't have to. The beginning of my life began when I came to believe that a power greater than myself, a God of my understanding, could restore me to sanity." He knows what it is to act and have an effect. I would surely put this man on my list as one of the most powerful people I know.

Like Tom, I made a choice. The choice I made should be obvious, because if I hadn't, I wouldn't be here today, doing what I'm doing, happy, joyous, and free. Now, I understand that it took every moment in time, every occurrence, every feeling, and every thought to bring me to the point of opening my mind to the possibility of a Higher Power from a totally new perspective. I could not go back and change the past, but I could change my perspective on the past, and how it led me to the present.

Tom myself, and scores of others like us came to believe that a power greater than ourselves could restore us to sanity . . . and it happened.

Step 3

We made a decision to turn our will and our lives over to the care of God as we understood God.

It has always amazed me that a room full of people from diverse backgrounds, male and female, of different races and of all religions and beliefs, are able to put their differences aside for the common cause of living in recovery from addiction in a 12-step meeting. It is not uncommon to see a doctor sitting next to a ditchdigger, a waitress laughing with a corporate executive, or a football player sharing with a housewife.

We are not people who would mix well in life, or even encounter each other, but for that one hour in a 12-step meeting, we are simply people seeking relief from addiction. And not only relief, but so much more: a healthier, happier way to live our lives. Therefore, those of us who are serious about working a 12-step program must leave our ego, self-centeredness, and need for control over others outside the door.

Our common problem brings us together, and sharing the struggle bonds us. But the spiritual experience is personal. I recently heard Pat H. say, "There's only two things I need to know about God. There is a God, and I'm not it." It doesn't matter what you call your Higher Power, or how you communicate with it. What's important is that you are willing to understand that you aren't running the show. Your best efforts landed you in a 12-step meeting, so whatever you were doing wasn't working, or you wouldn't be there.

Step 3 can be a stumbling block for many in the early days of recovery. Ruthy B. accompanied a friend, who she knew had a problem with addiction, to a 12-step meeting, just for support. Silently, she sat through the meeting and listened to others share their stories. Upon arriving home that night, she began to weep, as if someone had died. She said, "There was something about that place, the people, their stories, that made me understand it's where I belonged. All my life I wanted to belong somewhere, to be a part of the world, to fit in. I knew I was like those people." She returned to the meetings on her own.

Through the meetings, and the support of other addicts, Ruthy's life was getting better, but there was still something missing. When she was faced with step 3, she couldn't get past the questions in her mind: *If God is so great, if what they are saying about God's being loving, forgiving, and wonderful is true, why have I been given the life I've had?*

Once, in my early recovery, I voiced the same question. Jack C. responded by saying, "Do you think you're so special that you should be exempt from life's problems and tragedies? Do you think you are better than the rest of us? Why not you?" That was the last time I had to ask that question. Asked, and answered!

As Ruthy continued to attend meetings, she realized others were moving to places she could only imagine. She wanted what they had. She sought answers, but she kept running headlong into step 3. Until she was ready to open her mind to the possibility that a Higher Power could help her as it had helped others, she would remain unchanged.

The concept of *surrender*—for me and for many others like Ruthy—is difficult. Addicts, as a rule, live in a survivor mode for so long, attempting to control everything around them, protecting themselves from reality through addictions, that the word *surrender* is synonymous with giving up. Again, questions form in their minds. *What will happen if I give up what little control I have in life? What if I don't like God's idea of how I should be, how I should live? What if I can't handle the real world without a buffer?*

However, there are other questions that slip in under the radar. *What if it works? What if there is a plan? What if I try it for one day and see how it works?* Those questions are the crack in an otherwise closed mind; that is the beginning of spiritual exploration.

Step 3 tells you to turn your will and life over to a God of your understanding. It doesn't say to tell this God what to do and how to do it. If you pray that way, you will surely end up disappointed and believe the step doesn't work. The step will make no difference in your life unless you work it as stated. It is not something you do just once and then you're good. You must work step 3 on a daily basis if you are to reap the benefits of a spiritual life.

What happens when you are actually able to turn your will and life over to a God of your understanding on a daily basis? You will never be alone again. You will know self-worth and a sense of belonging. You will come to understand that no matter what life brings your way, it will always be for your best in the long run. Knowing these things will change your perception of yourself, others, and the world around you. With a God of your understanding in your corner, there is nothing you can't handle. That's not to say that once you learn to work step 3 each day, life will be all peaches and cream. Life keeps happening whether you are in your addictions or in recovery.

My dear friend Ruthy B. made the decision to work step 3. She told me, "At first, I wasn't always sure what I was supposed to do, but I had no doubt what I wasn't supposed to do: I wasn't supposed to step backward. If I kept moving forward, even if it was a baby step each day, and continued to turn my life over, I just knew everything would be OK."

I've watched her deal with great loss, serious illness, and horrendous pain, both emotional and physical, but she never wavers from the person I know her to be. She is as kind, loving, compassionate, and forgiving as the God of her understanding. Her humble selflessness extends far beyond a 12-step meeting to the world around her. She is an activist for abused animals. She said, "When I look into the eyes of an animal who has been abandoned, lost, or hurt, I know how they feel, and I want to help make them feel like the God of my understanding has made me feel—that I am important enough for someone to care."

I've also been fortunate enough to share in Ruthy's miracles. As a young girl, Ruthy gave up a child for adoption. This act preyed on her mind for years. She needed release from the feelings surrounding the situation and finally turned the issue over to the God of her understanding. She didn't ask God to return her daughter, to find a way for her to make it right; rather, she turned the issue over completely and let it go, knowing that whatever was right for her, and for her daughter, would happen.

Thirty years after she gave her daughter up, through a set of strange circumstances, mother and daughter were reunited, and they continue to have a relationship to this day. What an absolute miracle.

As is true of so many other things in life, we don't get what we need until we are willing to give up what it is we believe we want. Years ago I heard a woman say, "Why would I keep praying for a Volkswagen? God may want me to have a BMW. But as long as I keep telling him what to do, even if he does it I will sell myself short."

That's what step 3 is really about. It's about making a decision each day to surrender our lives to the Higher Power of our choosing, and accepting life on life's terms, knowing everything is as it should be. It's about never settling for being anything less than what God wants us to be, for having anything less than what God wants us to have. When I believed that through surrender I would be plagued with limitations, I was wrong. Through step 3, all the limitations I'd placed on myself were removed.

If someone had told me twenty-five years ago, when I began my recovery from addiction, where I would be today, I would have laughed in that person's face and said it was impossible. The God of my understanding had a plan for me, and it was way beyond my capabilities alone. Everything I am, everything I do, is a direct result of the day I decided to give up and allow my Higher Power to lead the way every day.

Step 4

We made a searching and fearless moral inventory of ourselves.

Others often ask me why I continue to attend meetings after so many years. There are many reasons, but one of the most important is that I am on a path of continual discovery of myself and other people. I will be a human being as long as I live, and I never know where, from whom, or how I will be given a message that will help me along this human path. I do know that if I don't put myself out into the world, with an open mind and a willingness to learn, the messages will escape me.

Jessica—young enough to be my granddaughter, still in a treatment center for her addictions, and less than thirty days into recovery—said, "When I'm in pain, I cause you pain." In all my years of recovery, I'd never heard those words spoken in quite that way. I needed to hear them that day. Over the past few months I'd been dealing with a person who was beginning to lean on my last nerve. I was suffering from frustration; I became angry, found myself judging the other person harshly, and was well on my way to resentment. Like I said, I will be human as long as I live.

I don't know how Jessica's words affected anyone else in the meeting, but they forced me to take an inventory of the situation, and of myself, before I did anything destructive to myself or the other person involved. The truth was that the woman was not doing what I suggested, the way I thought she should, in a timely manner. What was I thinking? Had I fallen back into ego so far that I believed I knew what was best for another human being, that I had the right to put expectations on her—unrealistic expectations? No! The negative thoughts and emotions that were starting to affect my life were not her fault. They were mine, and I had a choice to sit in them, let them build and devour me, or take an honest, fearless inventory and gain a new, healthier perspective. Through Jessica's words, I chose the latter.

I've read that step 4 is like running a business, and I've heard others make the same comparison. Isn't that what recovery is about: the business of living? Anyone who has run a business knows the importance of an accurate inventory. You can't know where you are if you don't know what you have and its cost. You can't know what you need until you understand which things are outdated and need to be discarded and replaced. It's only common sense.

A 12-step recovery program isn't simply about freedom from the addiction, but also about figuring out who you are, what brought you to the addiction, and those things that have the power to keep you running back to the addiction. Jean J. said, "Even though I hadn't indulged in my addiction in years, the disease went on without me and waited patiently for me to catch up. I did." Fear, guilt, shame, and worrying about what others might think of her if they knew the truth had kept Jean from doing a searching and fearless step 4.

It took being diagnosed with a brain tumor for Jean to become willing to do whatever it took—even the dreaded fourth step. She said, "At first, I thought I could soft-pedal it. Surely I didn't have to tell everything: how I'd lied and cheated; was self-centered, irresponsible, and totally self-absorbed. However, when I reflected back, I realized that it hadn't worked for me before. What made me think it would work this time? No, I'd have to do it fearlessly and completely, holding nothing back."

Jean survived the brain tumor, checked into a treatment facility, and sought out a sponsor who could help guide her through a thorough fourth step. The sponsor suggested that she first take a look back and write out events, situations, and relationships important in her life, what her feelings were, and where she placed the blame. She said, "It was easy for me to write about what others did to me, how situations affected me, and the unfairness of it all. Anger and resentments poured out onto my paper. Later, as I went back to read it, I realized how many of my life experiences I believed were the result of the thoughts and actions of others."

Her sponsor said, "What was your part in it? Step 4 is about cleaning up the wreckage of your past."

When addicts are faced with that one question, and are desperate enough to dig deep, pull out all that god-awful stuff that has lived in them and grown like a cancer, and look for their part in all situations, they have truly begun step 4. However, they have just begun.

Jean said her sponsor told her that working the fourth step was like peeling an onion. After she wrote things out, she was to give it a few days and then go back and look at what she'd written. If she needed to add more, that was the time to do it. Step 4 would be a process of peeling back the layers of her life until she reached the core. In the process, she was to remember that it was not about blaming others or herself; rather, it was about having an honest awareness of her life. How had she allowed other people, places, and things to affect her, and how did she act or react?

You'd better get out a lot of paper, because to success-fully work step 4 you will be looking at everything from legal issues, employment, family dynamics, and finances to relationships and sex—fearlessly. *Fearlessly* means just that. The very things you fear revealing the most are the most important things you need to face.

In the process of step 4, my sponsor used the phrase "bru-tal honesty" many times. Did he think I was a liar? I wonder why. There's an old joke that goes, "How do you know when an addict is lying?" The punch line is: "When their mouth is moving." Yes, I was a liar, and in the beginning I carried that into my recovery. For instance, because I didn't want anyone to know that my Grandpa Frank was the town drunk and that other family members were considered white trash, I said I didn't have any family—that they were all dead.

One day, after a meeting, a woman walked up to me and said, "Aren't you Eadie's granddaughter?" The jig was up. It was the first big lie I was caught in, but not the last. I suffered embarrassment, but the world didn't come to an end. No one, as I might have imagined, treated me any differently. Actually, I felt some relief when the truth came out. I stopped worrying about when, and how, it would happen.

It takes a lot of time and energy to be the great protector of your secrets. I was told that I am only as sick as my secrets. I used to wonder why my childhood friend Marsha, who was raised Catholic, went to confession. Now I understand. She wasn't in that little booth telling her priest about what other people did; she confessed her own actions. There's something about admitting the thoughts, feelings, and actions that belong to us; that way, they don't grow into the secrets that can ultimately ruin our lives.

There are many ways to work step 4, but all I can share with you is how I did it, and the fact that it worked for me. To stimulate my memory, I drew a life graph by years. Good years peaked upward, bad years plunged downward, and years when not much happened were a straight line. The way I'd lived wasn't conducive to straight lines, so it was mostly peaks and valleys. I think I had to have drama in my life to know I was alive.

Once I'd gotten pen to paper and then looked at my graph, I began writing, beginning with the most recent year, what happened, who was involved, how I felt about things then, and how I felt about them at the moment. I worked my way backward, peeling the onion layer by layer. Believe me, it was a big onion, with a lot of layers.

Like Jean, I had no trouble writing about others—the words and actions of theirs that had an effect on my life. Looking at my part in all situations was a whole different story. I think that's why the word *searching* is in step 4.

It was time for me to explore the deepest recesses of myself—that dark place where I kept the truth hidden behind a wall of addictions. It was frightening, because I was afraid once that door was open, what was behind it would surely kill me. However, if there was any hope for me, I would have to walk through the fear to the other side. The words *searching* and *fearless* played through my mind.

The investigation began. The most difficult truth I wrote about concerned my oldest son, Jon. The ramifications of one of the many things I did to him didn't show themselves until he was in his teens. When he was still a toddler, I told some lies, and made some serious threats, to keep his father from him. I dragged him through a life constantly on the run and kept him from close relationships with others. I made him believe, as I did at the time, that all we needed was each other, that there was nothing we couldn't overcome.

As children have a way of doing, he got older and began to have thoughts of his own. One of them was that he wanted to find his dad. Instead of understanding his need and supporting him, I told him even more lies. I was so focused on myself—my needs, my pain—that I couldn't see what was happening to him. He was well into his own addictions before I realized there was a problem. He stole a car, thinking he would drive it across country to find his dad. He was caught and thrown in jail.

I worked out a deal with the powers that be so he could go to long-term treatment instead of doing time in jail. Because he was only fifteen, they agreed. Jon was on probation, so if he left treatment he would have to serve his time in jail. He took off as soon as the opportunity arose and made his way to Arizona, still in search of his father. Shortly thereafter, I was informed that my son was dead. He'd been killed crossing Central Avenue in Phoenix.

All along, I'd blamed my family for not being supportive of me: my mother for taking her own life, Jon's dad for not loving me, God for killing my other children, and now Jon and all other human beings who had crossed my path and who did not live up to what I expected of them, who were not able to give me what I needed to be happy. It was all about me: my feelings, my pain, the unfairness of my life. Even my addictions were justified as I blamed others and my situations.

What was my part in the events that led to my son's death? To say I was selfish and self-absorbed is an understatement. I wanted Jon all to myself. Therefore, I alienated everyone else from our lives. I deluded myself into believing I was protecting him from others who might hurt him the way I'd been hurt, and from a cruel world, but the truth was that I needed him, his love and devotion, and did not want to share him with anyone else. I taught him, through example, how to be an addict and a runner, thumbing his nose at society, laws, and moral values. Then I berated him for being the very things I taught him to be. I set us apart from the world and then wondered why we felt as if we didn't fit in.

Jon went in search of a father he couldn't remember, in the hope of filling his needs—the ones I was incapable of filling. As difficult as it was to admit, I needed him; I took from him all he had to give, and I had nothing to give back. As I reflect in brutal honesty, even his death was not about him. It was about me: my pain, my loss, and another excuse to remain addicted.

Step 4 is the fourth step because without understanding my addictions and how they affected my life, without finding a support system and a Higher Power, there's no way I could have faced the truth about who I'd been and what I'd done. Neva G. reminded me that I was not a bad person trying to be good but a sick person trying to get better and that the fourth step was not about blame but about facing the truth so that I could move on.

This step will be an arduous, painful journey, but it is essential for those serious about recovery from addiction and searching for a better way of life. There are many opinions about whether it's best for a person to work step 4 just once or to return to it from time to time. It was suggested to me that if I worked my fourth step thoroughly, completely, holding nothing back, and used the maintenance steps, which I will address later in the book, I should never have to do it again. That worked best for me, but I am of the opinion that each person should do what works best for her.

If you believe that this step can be skimmed over, skipped, or done in half measures, be advised that you will be the one who pays the price. Even if you are able to keep whatever your addiction is at bay, the price could be falling into another addiction, living an unhappy life in recovery, or possibly slipping back into your old ways. Recovery is not just about the absence of your addiction; it is also about figuring out the causes, which will become clear if and when you are willing to work step 4.

Step 5

We admitted to God, to ourselves, and to another human being the exact nature of our wrongs.

My first thoughts when I encountered step 5 were: *You have got to be kidding. I'm not doing that. I wrote all my crap down, so why do I have to say it out loud? I don't believe these people "really" did that. If I was dying, I wouldn't tell anyone else all my stuff.*

To be able to maintain an addiction, an addict must be able to play many parts. It is important to convince others you are OK while you are dying inside, filled with fear, guilt, and shame. If you are a very good actor or actress, you may even be able to convince yourself at times. You might actually delude yourself into believing you are OK and in control, which will allow the addiction to escalate.

After you've had that moment of truth, hit bottom, and sought help in a 12-step meeting, don't imagine you will immediately let go of that side of your nature. You've cultivated it, nurtured it, even brought it to the point of an art form, and it is where you feel most comfortable. Changing will be a process. That's why there are twelve steps instead of just one.

In the beginning, I said things I thought others in the meetings wanted to hear. As I stuck around, I heard others doing the same thing. I knew what they were doing, and then I began to wonder if they were aware of what I was up to. Jack C. told me, "Bring the body, and the mind will follow." I didn't understand fully, but I kept going to the meetings. After a while, I began to notice the absence of some of the people I knew had been merely giving lip service to the program. When those individuals returned, broken, bruised, and beaten down by their addictions, their stories had changed dramatically. That got my attention.

Many said they'd worked the first four steps and then either refused to do, or put off doing, step 5. Some thought they could coast through the program without getting into any of the real action that is required to get through step 5. Others confided that they'd not been honest and thorough when they attempted step 5. My body had been sitting in meetings for some time, but now my mind was beginning to get the message. If I was going to get anywhere in my recovery and not slip back into my addictions, it would be essential that I actually work step 5.

Patrick C. was a coaster who had given half measures to step 5 during ten years in recovery from alcoholism. He'd brought his double life into the meetings: he looked good, said the right things, and did the mental steps, but he was unwilling to complete step 5. His program of recovery was stuck. After a time, his body not in the meetings, his mind began to wander back to old ways of thinking, to the delusions that enabled him to drink. He said, "A car accident got me on painkillers, and when they were gone, I returned to alcohol."

That might sound like a valid excuse to drink. However, those who understand the importance of step 5 understand that it is about burning bridges and knowing there is no excuse left to return to addiction. As a rule, addicts don't burn their bridges well, in case they need to go back. Therefore, for those who refuse to work step 5, it's easier to go back. For those who give step 5 half measures, they are simply waiting for a good excuse. For those who are waiting, an excuse will always present itself.

Nearly a year later, on the Fourth of July, Patrick came to in his home disarrayed by a month of neglect. He said, "For a month, I'd fallen hard off the wagon. I would awaken sometime in the a.m., get up as best I could, and stumble to the front door to check the porch. Hidden behind the post would be a bottle of vodka, delivered by a cabbie I'd paid off to keep me in alcohol. But that day was different.

"I did not look for that fresh bottle," he continued, "even though I needed that first drink of the day badly. That first drink—when I would manage, after several tries, to get it down and keep it down, I could spend the remainder of the day nibbling at the bottle, mindlessly watching television and drifting in and out of an alcohol-induced slumber. But that day, for whatever reason, I got up and stood before a crucifix on the wall of the living room. I was sick as I'd ever been. I was a mess—hadn't shaved, bathed, or brushed my teeth for a month. I'd lost over fifteen pounds on my drinking man's diet and was probably close to alcohol psychosis. I fell to my knees to pray. I fell flat on my face. As I lay there, all I could think of was to pray to God that if I had to live like this, I wouldn't die like this."

With the help of his wife, who was apparently a very forgiving, compassionate woman, he didn't drink that day. He returned to the 12-step meetings. He said, "It was relatively easy to go back to the program, but this time I knew I would have to do it differently. Based on previous attempts, I knew the fifth step would be one of the most difficult for me to accomplish as well as I needed. I could carry on conversations with most anyone, but I was always troubled with confiding deep inner feelings. Raised a Roman Catholic, I even had problems with the sacrament of confession. Ah, but step 5, admitting to another human being the exact nature of my wrongs. . . . I knew deep down, where I rarely ever go, that I had to do it right if I was ever ready to move on."

It's one thing to sit in the privacy of your living space, admitting to yourself, and to the God of your understanding, the exact nature of your wrongs, and a whole other thing to say it out loud to another human being. For me, it was like standing naked before the world with all my flaws hanging out for everyone to see. Talk about stepping out of my comfort zone! As much as I hate to admit it, I thought that if anything could drive me back to my addictions, it would be step 5.

Dwight S. explained to me that if I have truly worked the first four steps, have come to believe in a Higher Power and am able to turn my will and life over to my Higher Power every day, it sets the foundation for me to be capable of working step 5. I would not be walking through the fear, the shame, the guilt, alone.

Whom would you trust with all your dirty little secrets? If you are involved in organized religion, you might choose a priest or minister. If not, you might do your fifth step with a trusted friend, a family member, or another member of your 12-step group. You must remember that whomever you choose, it should be someone who will not be adversely affected by your confessions, and it should be a person who is open-minded about the process—what you are doing, and why.

It would be inappropriate to choose a person who could be devastated by your confession—someone who loves you and has already suffered through your addictive behavior. It would be foolish to choose a person from the clergy whom you know to be judgmental and closed-minded about addiction. It would be ineffective to choose a friend or another 12-step member who tends toward enabling others, who thinks taking step 5 is simply tea and conversation. This is serious business that will have a great impact on your path of recovery.

Patrick C. said, "My sponsor, a good guy and a great sponsor, was always there for me. He understood the power of alcoholism, and the resultant problems. He was not, however, the person I needed to do the fifth step with. It would have been too easy—another mini-meeting over a long lunch and coffee. It was not the time for the softer, easier way.

"Old Ray, a retired gentleman with a lively disposition, was at almost every meeting I attended, and probably many I didn't. Ray was an eloquent speaker, but underlying all the rhetoric, I sensed his hard-nosed attitude toward life and recovery. Instinctively, I knew he was my guy."

For Patrick, who was serious about doing step 5 to the best of his ability, it was important to choose a person who had truly walked the path he wished to walk, who knew the importance of brutal honesty and thoroughness when working step 5—and who would not let him skim over or skip any part of his experiences, or make light of what he'd done.

When you choose that person with whom you will do step 5, there are other things to consider. You'll want to find a place of privacy, with no distractions, one that is comfortable—because if you are like most addicts, it could take a while. Turn off the music, the television, and the telephone;

if there are children and pets, make sure they are taken care of; and if there is coffee or other refreshments, make sure they are already made. You are ready to begin.

Some people begin by allowing the other person to read what they have written in step 4. Others simply begin at the beginning and relate their story, leaving nothing out. Because this can be a very emotional encounter, it is usually wise to avoid public places like restaurants. You may be surprised at the tears that well up, the sadness and anger that you feel, and the foul words that come out of your mouth as you proceed.

The exact nature of your wrongs? That's tough. You must put aside blaming others or attempting to justify your actions or reactions to others, and tell the absolute truth about your part in each situation. One of the most difficult parts of step 5 for me was talking about my dad. Since childhood, I blamed him for abandoning me to my addicted mother and cruel stepfather. He was supposed to protect me, to save me from the life I was forced to live, and he didn't. How did I react to that? I withheld my affection and did everything I could to make his life miserable. When my mother killed herself and he attempted to reach out to me, I spewed venom and blamed him.

Later on, when I moved away to another state, he reached out again. He said he wanted to talk to me. He wanted to see me, and I agreed to a certain date. The day he arrived, after driving cross-country, I was gone. Feeling very proud of myself and totally justified, with nothing more than a desire to hurt him, I got on an airplane and flew away.

That was a small example of the hateful, mean-spirited things I did to hurt him and others. My mother used to say, "You would cut off your nose to spite your face." She wasn't wrong, but it wasn't until I worked steps 4 and 5 that I came to understand the meaning of her words. The hardest admission I had to make was that I'd put unrealistic expectations on my father, thinking he had control over things he had no control over; that I loved him deeply but feared that love, feared loss, feared pain; that I was filled with fear. That was hard to admit because I came across to others like I was tough, unaffected, and feared nothing and nobody. The facade was beginning to slip.

The way I'd lived, image was everything. But inside quivered a mass of raw nerves terrified that someone would figure me out, get to know the real person. Step 5 is about removing the mask, letting go of the image, getting real, and taking responsibility. Through step 5, I understood who I was, what I'd done, and how I'd rationalized my actions.

Patrick C. said it best when he said, "Through step 5, I underwent a complete catharsis. I knew if I continued doing the next right thing, everything would be all right. It was as though a huge roadblock had been lifted from my life and I was now free to proceed on to better things. The anxiety and guilt I'd kept inside all those years was gone. I felt like I was breathing fresh air for the first time in so long. It was the beginning of my honesty with myself, and others, that has allowed me to get past the past and on to the good life I enjoy today."

Unlike Patrick, I never actively returned to my addictions, although I came close at times; but like him, for me step 5 was the key to opening the floodgates of the past, letting everything out, so I could move on in my recovery and my life in a happier, healthier way.

When you reach step 5 and realize how difficult it may be for you, there can be a myriad of excuses not to do it. I've heard them all—and have thought of a few myself.

EXCUSE	TRUTH
EXCUSE: I'm not ready.	**TRUTH:** You don't want to put yourself through it.
EXCUSE: I don't know anyone I trust that much.	**TRUTH:** You need to actively find someone; if you really want recovery, you will have to trust someone someday.
EXCUSE: I don't have the time right now.	**TRUTH:** You make time for what is important.
EXCUSE: I can do it later.	**TRUTH:** Later may never come if you return to your addiction.

As daunting as step 5 may seem, this is not the time for procrastination. If you want an excuse to avoid it, you will find one. Addicts are really good at that. If you are interested in recovery from your addiction, you will, as my friend Antonio always says, "Get into action." The benefit you derive from working step 5 will be a direct result of your willingness to expose yourself fully, completely, and honestly to God, yourself, and another human being.

Steps 6 & 7

We were entirely ready to
have God remove all these defects
of character.

·

We humbly asked God to
remove our shortcomings.

There was a time, after my release from a mental institution, when I was given an opportunity through the state of Illinois to have therapy and get an education. I knew it would be the answer to my problems. I wanted to understand my addictive behavior and learn new coping skills. It would open a whole new world of ideas and people for me. I was like a sponge, sucking up all the information I could gather.

It was during that time that I first heard of a 12-step program. Money being in short supply, I lived in a motel room, converted into a studio apartment, with my son, another girl, and a dog. A man that lived two doors down, a fellow student and in recovery from addiction, attempted to share with me the advantages of working the steps. Phillip S. said, "If psychology, medicine, and religion worked, we wouldn't have therapists, doctors and nurses, or priests and ministers sitting in meetings."

I argued that there were always some weak-minded people who couldn't do it on their own, but I wasn't one of them. Once, I'd heard a therapist-teacher say, "Addicts may as well thumb their noses at the rest of us and say that they are special, different, that they shouldn't have to cope with life's problems like the rest of us. Then they whine on about not feeling like they fit in. Who do they think they are?" I shared this with Phillip. He shook his head and said, "Until you find faith, find a way to put your past to rest, and confront your defects of character, your addiction will live on."

What defects of character? I was fine: I was not indulging my addictions; I was in therapy and getting educated. He was brainwashed by those 12-step people. It was just crazy talk. My faith was in my intellectual ability to beat this addiction thing, and what happened before didn't matter.

Some years later, my addictions reared their ugly heads again. I hit bottom and begged those people in a 12-step group to help me—you know, those ones I'd judged as weak-minded individuals. My brief encounter with Phillip came back to haunt me when I read step 6. I realized that throughout the time I considered myself recovered from my addiction, I continued to hold on to my defects of character.

I considered the words of the therapist-teacher I'd quoted to Phillip. I'd agreed with the man, but as I looked back, I saw that I'd deluded myself into believing he wasn't talking about me—that I was smart, strong, and had it all figured out. Questions arose. Had I been so self-involved that I didn't think trauma, tragedy, and living problems are a part of every person's life if they live long enough? Did I not comprehend that others found a way to cope without escaping into addictions and creating the chaos that seemed to follow me around like my own personal black cloud, setting me apart from the rest of humanity? Did it make me feel different, special—and did I use that as a justification to act out in inappropriate ways?

As I pondered these questions, not yet ready to accept the truth of some of my character defects, I heard Elmer, who was having his three-year recovery anniversary, say, "I had the strangest encounter with my oldest son." Elmer, who had thrived in his addictions for years, who had been neglectful of his family, wanted to mend fences, but his oldest son was not ready to trust him. "They were having a cake at my home meeting to celebrate my anniversary," he continued, "and I wanted my family to be there. My oldest son told his mother he didn't want to go. I went to speak to him, to tell him how important it was to me. I poured my heart out to him. He sat there and stared at me until I finished. Then he said, "When is mom's party?" Stunned, I didn't get it for a minute. When I did, it was the most humbling experience of my life."

While Elmer had spent his time seeking addictions that enabled him to escape, his wife, one way or another, had dealt with his addictive behavior, working, raising the kids, facing every one of the problems he refused to deal with. And Elmer, like me, could not see past his own nose, or his pain, to the truth.

The brief encounter with Phillip S., the therapist's words, and Elmer's story brought on my big epiphany as I considered my character defects. Suddenly I realized that the one character defect that all addicts have in common is self-centeredness. The rest of the defects of character stem from it. The self-centered are concerned totally with their own desires, needs, and interests and are oblivious to the needs and feelings of others. This was not what I wanted to believe about myself, but the truth was the truth no matter how I tried to spin it.

I still wasn't "entirely" ready to admit, accept, and let go of my defects of character, but as I sat in the meetings and listened to the stories of others, I came to understand that until that happened, one of two things might occur. Either I would live without my addictions in a state of misery, or I would return to them.

When Mike E. came to in a jail cell, desperate, believing he was going to die, he said to God, "I'll gladly exchange my life so the guy I ran over can live." Mike didn't die, and as soon as he was released, he returned to his addictions.

Months later, in court, he was given the choice between jail and a treatment center. He said, "I figured that compared to jail, treatment would be a cakewalk. I'd been there and done that, in short spurts, before."

However, Mike found himself not only in treatment but loaded on a bus with others like him and shipped off to 12-step meetings. He said, "As time passed, my mind cleared and I began to think about how I got to that point. What in the world happened to me that there was nothing left but character defects?"

As Mike shared the particulars of his story, it became clear that he had clung to his character defects, allowing them to affect his personal life, military service, work, and family, which caused him to feel like a failure—a "zero," as he put it—almost to the point of death. Those feelings of being a failure always brought him back to his addictions.

Step 6 was particularly poignant for Mike because he knew if he kept living, and thinking, the way he had, no matter what else was happening around him, the results would be the same. Another 12-step member suggested that he needed to be serious and sincere with step 6. Mike said, "When I'm tempted to be less than on the up-and-up, I am to remind myself of the price to be paid: guilt, shame, and remorse—which makes me irritable, restless, and discontent."

Like Mike, when I become irritable, restless, and discontent, I fall back on those defects of character that allow complete self-centeredness. I heard someone in a meeting call it "survival of the most self-involved." What in the world would I fall back on if I became "entirely" ready to have God remove "all" these defects of character? How would I survive? Maybe I could hold on to some of them. There might come a time when I would need to lie and to manipulate others, or a situation, to achieve my goals. Damn, that word *all* kept popping up.

I was told that if I was serious about step 6, there was no room for compromise. Doug D. said, "You can't horse-trade with God. He's got both horses." It seemed that it was all or nothing. If I was going to move on to step 7, I would have to become "entirely" ready to release "all" my defects of character. I knew that if I ever did that, my life would be forever changed, and I would never be able to go back again.

"Do you like yourself?" Neva G. asked me. "Do you like being a phony? Aren't you tired of keeping up the act?" I could feel the tears welling in my eyes. I was tired, so tired, so unhappy, and it wasn't that I didn't want to do things differently, but I didn't know how. "Why are you so afraid of letting go of the very things that are making you unhappy?" she continued. I didn't have an answer for her, but I took her words home with me, could not get them out of my mind, and sought her out the following day to tell her I believed I was entirely ready, and to ask what to do next.

"Your part in step 6 is to become ready. Are you ready?" Neva asked. I stared into my cup of coffee and nodded my head, afraid of what would come next. "Then, all you have to do is ask." That's it? That's all I have to do? Neva smiled, and said, "That's it. Step 7 tells you to ask God to remove your shortcomings." I could do that.

Later, in my recovery, Nancy O. said, "For years, my Higher Power, whom I choose to call God, drew huge pictures for me, but I would crash into them like the Roadrunner into an animated mountainside. Then I would grab on to my addictions and run off in another direction, searching, ever searching for the answers to life's questions for which there were no answers. At least there were no answers I could live with at the time."

Like me, Nancy had nurtured and cultivated her character defects, all the while blaming others and looking for answers outside herself. She said, "Promiscuity, all forms of addictions, rage, and suicide attempts plagued my life. I was like a self-absorbed tornado, ripping through the world and others, leaving nothing but destruction in my path—all the while trying to look good on the outside, even to the point of fooling myself."

Appearances can be deceiving. Nancy, like me and other addicts, held tight to those character defects that enabled her to live the lie, and the result was one addiction after another. I heard a guy named Joe say that swapping addictions is like changing seats on the *Titanic.* I knew he'd traveled the same path as I had.

I told myself I was searching for answers, but that wasn't true. No one who behaves the way I did, seeking one form of escape after another, wants answers. If I got answers, like I would if I worked the steps, I might feel as if I actually had to do something about myself and about the mess I'd made of my life and the lives of those who cared for me. Step 7 is the beginning of that realization. It was time to act, to ask my Higher Power to remove my shortcomings.

After Nancy became entirely ready and asked God to remove her shortcomings, she said, "I realized only the God of my understanding could alter my responses to life, from rage to acceptance. My instincts, gone astray, always produced humiliating behavior for me, all the way to years of incomprehensible demoralization. I'd been blessed with experience after experience after humiliating experience, in and out of addiction, before I'd become aware of the depths of my character defects. The insanity of my inability to change my behavior was terrifying and unbearable.

"Step 7 allowed me to become humbled and to recognize my humanity. It is what provides me with the evidence that my understanding of a God in my life is evolving. The results of my actions and my thoughts prove the process of removal of my character defects. I am able to place this God between me and people, places, and things throughout the day."

Jack C. once said to me, "I couldn't, He could. So why not ask Him?" I did.

The proof is in the pudding, as they say. The changes in my life—not only in the way I live, but in the way I think and feel—have been drastic since I made the decision to become entirely willing to let God remove all my defects of character and then asked God to remove them. The roadblocks that kept me in my addictions and misery were lifted so that I could become the person I always (secretly) wanted to be. You see, during all those years when I was making fun of others who didn't think and act like me, the truth was that I was envious because I didn't think I could have what they had. I couldn't figure out how to get where they were. Like a child that envies another's toy, if I couldn't have it, I attempted to destroy it. I didn't know why I did those things, and I couldn't figure out a way to stop, until I encountered steps 6 and 7. The God of my understanding has done for me what I could not do for myself. God has removed from me all those things that stood in the way of my having the best life I can have, of being the person God always knew I could be. And all I had to do was ask.

Steps 8 & 9

We made a list of all persons we had harmed, and became willing to make amends to them all.

·

We made direct amends to such people wherever possible, except when to do so would injure them or others.

If you have worked the steps in the order in which they are written, two things should have occurred to help you move on to step 8: honesty and awareness. However, even with honesty and awareness, steps 8 and 9 will be no walk in the park. These steps are about putting into actions all those things you have written about, talked about, and prayed about. All your thoughts and words, written or spoken, will mean nothing until you find the willingness to back them up with action.

Roxy G. said, "I spent many glorious years in a 12-step program until I ran into step 8. I thought I'd never hurt anyone. They'd all hurt me. They abandoned me. They neglected me. They abused and molested me. I was just a kid. They were in the wrong. I was completely innocent, doing what I had to, to survive. All they ever gave me was pain and misery."

By age sixteen, a victim of domestic violence and physical, sexual, and spiritual abuse, Roxy packed an army bag and took refuge on the streets. She slept in the gutted-out trunk of a car, in parks, or anywhere else available to keep her out of the elements. She gave birth to a baby boy but continued living the same way until she became so desperate that she cried out to, as she put it, a God of which she "had no understanding," and begged for help.

Roxy met a man in a 12-step program who introduced her to a way of recovery from her many addictions. She thrived in the program, getting her life together—until she faced step 8.

It's difficult, after many years of blaming others to justify addictions and addictive behavior, to accept that maybe we had something to do with what happened to us. Like addictions, old habits die hard. But die they must if we are to have the life we desire: a life free not only of our addictions but of our past. Steps 8 and 9 are intended to clean up the wreckage of *our* past, not the indiscretions of others.

Roxy said, "Through others in recovery, I began to see things through new eyes. I was not always the victim. Many times, I volunteered to allow others to treat me badly. I'd done things for others not out of the goodness of my heart, but with secret agendas and for covert reasons. If I was nice to them, they would have to be nice to me. I can't tell you how many men I went through while believing that if I loved them good, they would treat me good and not leave me. I didn't do anything just because I wanted to, or for altruistic reasons. Any kindness I showed had underlying, selfish motives."

It's called the "What's in it for me?" game. I played it for years, even in early recovery. I was looking for payback for all those wrongs, real and imagined, that I believed had been thrust upon me. I thought everyone owed me something and that anything I did was OK, because, like Roxy, I believed I hadn't had the life I should have lived. The new awareness was that things were what they were, that I couldn't go back and change them. I'd made choices, many not so wise, in my actions and reactions to other people, and it was time to take a hard look at those choices . . . and make my list.

Addicts live in extremes, need drama to know they are alive, and spend a lot of time and effort trying to recapture that first high. That attitude carried through as I made my list. Once I began, it became a list that would rival Santa's good-boy, bad-boy lists. Then I was told that's not what it's about. To set myself an impossible task of looking up every waitress I'd been nasty to, every person I'd stolen from, those who had been on the receiving end of my vicious tongue, those with whom I'd committed numerous indiscretions, was to set myself up for failure.

Neva G. said, "You need to concern yourself with those people you've harmed that live within you. They are the things that bother your mind, that you take to bed at night, that, if you are honest, are shrouded in shame and guilt, because you know somewhere in the deepest part of you, you did the wrong thing. It doesn't matter what 'they' did, whether you instigated the problem or simply reacted to it. How did you act? How has that affected you?" I eliminated a lot of names, but it was still a pretty hefty list.

The second half of step 8 says, "became willing to make amends to them all." I didn't know about that. I understood the importance of making amends for those situations I'd caused, but I was still bothered by the idea of making amends to those who had harmed me. What to do? A friend, a 12-stepper herself, shared with me that she hung her list of those who had harmed her up where she would have to see it every day, and each morning she prayed for the willingness to make amends. With two magnets, I stuck my list to the refrigerator. One day, a friend who had come for a visit stood looking at the list. She said, "Didn't you forget someone?" I couldn't imagine who that could be. She said, "Where's your name?"

That statement opened a whole new can of worms. Me? How do I make amends to myself? After she left, her words haunted me. The truth was that I'd done some pretty awful, self-destructive things to myself. I scribbled my name on the list. As I walked past my list one day, as yet incapable of putting it into action, I had a thought. Maybe I needed to start with myself, to practice making amends by looking in a mirror and saying the words out loud.

I faced the girl in the mirror, the girl whom I'd kept from the rest of humanity for fear of getting hurt; whom I dragged through addictions and bad relationships, in and out of self-destructive situations; whom I had been so cruel to. It was no wonder she hated me, and I apologized. The realization for me that day was that until I felt I was worthy of forgiveness, I couldn't go forward and seek forgiveness from others. It was the beginning of the willingness it would take for me to work step 9.

Even though Susan H. revealed her deepest, dark-est secret—that she had been an incest victim, her father the perpetrator—to another person during step 5, she was unable to see her part in it. After years in recovery from her addictions, and remarriage to another 12-step member, the trouble began.

She said, "Relationships, in particular with men, became strained and began to affect me at work and in my friend-ships. I became supersensitive. I felt victimized, taken advantage of, sometimes overlooked. I withdrew from social settings, feeling more and more isolated, even uncomfortable in 12-step meetings. I attended less and less. I pushed my husband away with outbursts of temper and incomprehensible emotional mood swings. I was angry, and all the things I'd used to stuff my feelings away—alcohol, work, food, sex—no longer worked. I was poised to run—to walk off my job, leave my husband, where I lived—but I stayed and raged on."

Addiction is about escape, so what are addicts to do when what they need to escape from lives within? No matter where they go, what they are doing, whom they are with, that need is there like a buzzing bee that just won't leave them alone. I've heard it said that resentments are a luxury addicts can't afford. A single resentment, held on to for too long, puts the addict in danger of relapse.

Continuing her story, Susan said, "I was unable to deal with my anger. It spewed out at the wrong times, directed at the wrong people. As when I was active in my addictions, others began to pull away. I felt alone, isolated, sorry for myself, and didn't know why. A relapse was just around the corner. When my dad became ill, I returned home. My old resentment resurfaced. I acted out—angry, disrespectful, and belligerent. I certainly wasn't the kind, caring daughter I believed I would be in recovery.

"I sought help from the woman who knew my secret. I asked her for help. She called my feelings, my behavior, by its right name: resentment, relived anger. She said I would not be free until I looked at my part in the situation. I was a child, a victim. What part could I have possibly played? I sought help from a professional. Through a group of others who'd lived through similar experiences, I realized some had found their way to forgiveness. Others held on to their pain, continuing to be a victim of the past. Their entire lives revolved around hating their perpetrators—anger and resentment. I was at a crossroads, faced with the choice of finding a way to forgive or continuing to harbor this huge resentment and playing the victim. I didn't know if I could forgive my father. More than any other experience in my life, what he'd done to me had altered the entire course of my life."

It is a difficult concept for us to grasp: that we addicts must find a way to forgive everyone everything, to apologize for our behavior to others who have hurt us so badly. However, that's what step 9 is about: no matter what others have done to us, to discover our part in it and make amends wherever possible.

Susan continued: "I prayed. I wrote. I cried. I stomped. I cursed. I read books. I shared at meetings, but only in a general way. Others who'd had similar experiences could hear what I wasn't saying and spoke to me after the meetings. They'd made peace with their past. Could I?... Was it possible? I attended more meetings and began to listen to others share how they'd come through horrible situations and had even been able to use them to benefit others.

"I opened my eyes one morning, and it seemed so clear. I understood my part in the situation. I had none! I was a child. I'd dragged something terrible from my childhood into adulthood and continued to harbor the same feelings I'd known as an abused child. I'd never come to understand that my father suffered from a soul sickness, was a broken man. I called him. It was time to work my ninth step with him."

Susan went to her father and saw him from a totally different perspective. He no longer seemed the formidable man she'd once known, but an old, sick, frail human being. She explained to him why she'd come.

Susan continued: "I told my father of the things that happened to me as a child that had changed my life. I had bad feelings toward him since, and I was sorry. I shared that even though he'd tried to do things for me, tried to make up for things in his own way, I'd been difficult. When kindness would have made life easier for all concerned, I raged on. I was sorry I'd caused upsets in the family while in my addictions, worried them, and continued my behavior in recovery. I asked for his forgiveness, and asked if we could let go of the past and move forward. He wept and apologized to me.

"I saw a sad old man with a broken spirit. I didn't know what happened to him in his past that broke something in him, but all I could feel at that moment was pity. I told him it would be OK. Over the next two years, I made an effort to spend time with him, to get to know him. I asked questions about his childhood, career, experiences—his life. I listened. I came to care deeply for, and forgave, this man . . . my father."

There will be many situations and people for which addicts must make their amends. Some people will react like Susan's father, others will not. The key to working step 9 is not to assume anything, but to go about the business of making amends wherever needed and allowing others to react however they choose. You should never put off making amends because you think you know how the other person will react. That is the other person's business and is between that person and her conscience.

When considering your amends, do not forget the second half of step 9. You are to do no further harm. Larry S. shared what he'd done to his ex-wife when he went to make amends—obviously, before he was completely ready. He said, "I didn't simply apologize to her for being unfaithful. I gave names, many of which were people still in her life, some related to her. I wanted to see the pain in her eyes. She'd left me, hurt me, and was having a good life without me . . . the one I thought I was supposed to have."

Larry hurt not only his ex-wife, but others involved. Later, when he became truly ready to make amends, he had a lot more people to face, and he was sure his ex-wife would never forgive him for what he'd done that cost her so dearly. Others have the right to their secrets, their choices in life, to face their truths when the time is right for them. That is not your business. You are to clean your side of the street without touching theirs.

One of the problems you might encounter is that those to whom you owe amends have moved away or died. There are solutions. I know that, because most of the important people in my life had left or died, and I owed all of them amends. You can use these circumstances as an excuse to avoid making the amends, which will only hurt you in the long run, or you can try some of the things that worked for me and others. For those who have moved away, you must do everything you can to locate them; if this is impossible, you can pray for forgiveness of your actions and hold tight to the willingness to make amends in case a new opportunity arises.

I'd been in recovery from my addictions for a number of years before I was given the opportunity to make my amends to a person I'd harmed greatly. A strange set of circumstances brought him back into my line of vision. I'd prayed for forgiveness of my transgressions against him, but it was nothing compared to that face-to-face meeting. You might be surprised to know that the other person involved was not at all receptive. Nevertheless, I pressed on, made my apologies, and knew peace. I wish I could have given this person peace, but that was not in my power.

I spent a lot of time visiting cemeteries, talking to headstones; writing letters to those who had died and burning them; praying for the forgiveness of the dead, hoping they heard me, could understand how sorry I was for those things I did to hurt them. I found peace through these actions. Step 9 means getting into action, making all amends, no matter how difficult, and doing everything within your power to complete the task without hurting others in the process.

If you are interested in resolving your past issues, in ridding yourself of resentments and anger, and are tired of carrying the past like a weight on your shoulders, the answer lies in step 9. In finishing her story, Susan H. said, "The gift of the ninth step came. I had a peace inside that I'd never known. A friend of my husband's told me not to have any 'I wish I woulda's' or 'If I had only's.' I didn't. My side of the street was finally clean. My heart was clear. There was no anger, no hidden resentments, no fear, no unfinished business."

Free at last!

Part II

the promises

We are going to know a new freedom and a new happiness.

We will not regret the past, nor wish to shut the door on it.

We will comprehend the word *serenity,* and we will know peace.

No matter how far down the scale we have gone, we will see how our experience can benefit others.

That feeling of uselessness and self-pity will disappear.

We will lose interest in selfish things and gain interest in our fellows.

Self-seeking will slip away.

Our whole attitude and outlook on life will change.

Fear of people and economic insecurity will leave us.

We will intuitively know how to handle situations that used to baffle us.

We will suddenly realize that God is doing for us what we could not do for ourselves.

Are these extravagant promises? We think not. They are being fulfilled among us—sometimes quickly, sometimes slowly. They will always materialize if we work for them.

—*Alcoholics Anonymous,* chapter 6

It's nine o'clock Sunday morning. At a small house in Wickenburg, Arizona, people from the United States, Canada, Europe, and Mexico arrive. One by one they enter, greet each other, and find a chair. The room is full. Some are sitting on a counter; others stand in the back of the room. I find a folding chair to one side where I can see everyone.

Some of the participants, like Heather B., a single mother of two little boys, work in one of the local treatment facilities. I've had the privilege of watching Heather change and grow into a beautiful person and a loving, active parent over the past three years. Back from the colder states are the snowbirds, some of whom I get to reunite with for a few months each year. There are groups of beginners, bused in from treatment centers, who clump together, sometimes holding each other's hands. I love to watch the bonds that form between some unlikely individuals from different states, countries, and stations in life. Then there are the locals, like me, who attend year-round. I'm not really a local, as I live on the top of a mountain nearly forty-five minutes away, but the Sunday-morning group is my home group.

Humanity is made up of many small groups of people with common goals. From street gangs to politicians, people find a group with whom they can relate. Within each group there are nuances—words and phrases that mean something only to its members.

In a recovery group, one of the phrases you will probably hear is "Welcome to Oz." It's used for those addicts who show up late for meetings, paste a smile on their faces, insist everything is fine, fine, fine, have nothing to add to the meeting, and leave early. It's not meant to be funny or a judgment; rather, it's about knowing what it is to live in delusion and denial. Many of the "Welcome to Oz" sayers started out the same way.

The Wizard of Oz tells the story of addiction. The illness began before the addiction. When the addiction took hold, the addicts rode it like a tornado until they ended up in an unfamiliar place. They didn't know where they were, how they got there, what they were doing, or where to go. The one thing they did know was that they were different from everyone else. They didn't belong.

When reality hits and the addict makes the decision to seek recovery from his addiction, it is like taking that first step on the Yellow Brick Road that will begin his journey home. There will be others in the 12-step meetings who will be on the same journey. And they are all off to meet the Wizard to find answers. They will become a group of seekers who will learn to care for each other, support one another, and encourage each other to continue the journey.

Like the Yellow Brick Road, the Twelve Steps of recovery will have many twists and turns, and will be fraught with unexpected hurdles. However, the seekers desire what is at the end of the road. Like the Lion, the Scarecrow, the Tin Man, and Dorothy, they want to be able to think and feel, to have courage and a place of peace where they feel at home.

Although they all feel as if they are searching for the Wizard for different reasons, it's all about self-esteem, self-respect, and being made whole. The Wizard is a God of their understanding, and when they find that God, they will discover that everything they sought has lived within them the entire time. They simply had to learn to tap into it.

It may seem odd to think of a 12-step meeting as home, but for those addicts who have suffered greatly, who have spent most of their lives feeling as if they were on the outside looking in, who believed there was no place for them in the world, that's exactly what it is: *home.* Home should be that place where people feel comfortable being exactly who they are, where others love them unconditionally, where they always know that no matter what happens, they are not alone and everything will ultimately be OK. Home is hope.

For the first time, addicts are in a place where they feel as if they belong, with others who understand and who know that, through the Twelve Steps, they will be guided to a better way of life. Each step brings them closer to their goal of being made whole. Then they will step out of Oz and into the real world, and know that it is where they belonged all along.

Through a program of recovery that uses the Twelve Steps, addicts learn about using their brains, hearts, and courage to live in the real world. Then, there are the "Promises." Are they extravagant promises? In the beginning, most addicts think the promises are impossible, that if they can simply find freedom from their addictions, getting through their days with some grace, it's probably more than they deserve. However, there is so much more.

We are going to know a new freedom and a new happiness.

Remove the addiction, and remove the excuses for destructive behavior. When addicts no longer need to lie, cheat, steal, manipulate, or live their lives around the addiction, they automatically experience a new freedom. For most, with that new freedom comes a conscience. From that moment on, they are responsible for every choice they make.

For addicts in recovery, does a conscience bring happiness? Through honest awareness of where they've been, what they've done, and who they became, and through working the Twelve Steps, addicts will be given the tools they need to resolve past issues that may have haunted them for years. They will gain an understanding that they are not "bad" people, but that they suffered from addiction, and it affected every facet of their lives.

Evelyne, a robust woman I met in a meeting, said, "People do the best they can with what they have to work with at the time. You can't expect them to do what they don't know how to do. Their best isn't always the greatest, but it's all they have until they learn a better way." You can't imagine how much that helped me with the negative feelings about my parenting that had haunted me for so long. Those important in my young life taught me, through their actions, how to cope with life. That's all I knew how to do at the time. However, with the steps as a guide, I could learn a better way to live.

For me, the new happiness was the discovery that I wasn't stupid, evil, a bad seed, or unteachable. There was hope that I could change my life. By the time I got into recovery, my kids were dead, and there was nothing I could do to help them. But there were things I could do to help others—maybe your child, or another parent without a clue. I could share my experience, strength, and hope with others and, like Evelyne, say something to another person struggling for recovery from addiction, something that can make a difference.

Happiness comes from knowing that I am exactly where I need to be, doing what I'm doing today, and that it took everything that happened in my life, every learning experience, to bring me to this point. It's a new point of view, one that convinces me that all the awful things that happened to me, and the terrible things I did, are not without merit if I can use them to help others. Mine was not a worthless life, as I once believed, but a life filled with opportunities to be taken when I became ready to see them. However, until I removed the addictions, I could not see past them to find clarity of mind, body, and spirit.

We will not regret the past, nor wish to shut the door on it.

Susan H. said, "My dark past has become one of my greatest assets. By sharing my experiences—and that's what they really are—simply one experience after another in my life, with both men and women, I have seen them come to a point of willingness to let go of the pain of the past, begin to heal, and find that peace which had eluded them for so long."

Amends have been made. Wounds are healing. The wreckage of the past has been put to rest through working the first nine steps of a 12-step program. However, no matter how much a person wishes to escape it, the past is a part of each individual, and to deny the past is to deny the truth. What is to be done with that concept?

It is the belief of many addicts in recovery that it took every moment in their lives, every experience that occurred, every person who passed through, to bring them to that one moment when they had a spiritual awakening. If that is true—and it certainly has been for me—then the past was not a waste or a bad thing, but a thing of value that can be used to understand and help those still in the grips of addiction. Because addicts in recovery have traveled the path before in overcoming their struggle with addiction, they are in the unique position of being able to say, "I understand. This is what I did that worked for me."

If I'm able to share with you, openly and honestly, stories about my past, you will be more prone to open yours to me. You will know that, given all the things I did in the throes of addiction, I will not judge you. Roxy G. said, "I came to believe I was not a bad person for having bad behavior. I am not my addictions, nor am I my past. I am who I am today, and it's about the value system I choose to live by at this moment in time. My self esteem is in direct proportion to how accountable I am for my choices."

We will comprehend the word serenity, *and we will know peace.*

I've heard it said that people are only as sick as their secrets. Addicts have an alternative personality that takes over when they are active in their addictions. That personality can do horrendous things—things that are totally out of character. Shame, guilt, and fear will push these things into the secretive world of the addict. What would others think of them if they knew the truth?

Secrets are like vampires. Once they are exposed to the light of day, they lose their power. In a 12-step meeting, which is a safe, nonjudgmental place for addicts, the secrets are revealed. Through the steps, the way to either fix or resolve all the pain addicts have caused themselves and others will become apparent. When that happens, addicts will not only live each day free of their addictions but come to know those first moments of peace, to begin to understand the word *serenity.* Serenity is utter calmness, and peace is the absence of stress.

It is an amazing day for addicts when they no longer carry the pain of the past or feel compelled to guard those god-awful secrets that could come out at any time to expose them and make them feel vulnerable. Once they've put it all out there and seen that the world didn't come to an end, that others didn't run away screaming, they can lie down at night without their minds taking them to strange places, and they can sleep like a child who feels safe and happy. They have found peace and serenity.

Coupled with the freedom from secrets is the belief that there is a Higher Power of the addicts' choosing who wants only the best for them. When a spiritual awakening takes place, two things happen: First, they come to realize they never have to walk alone again. Second, the newfound sense of belonging they've discovered in a 12-step program expands outward, first to their families, friends, and community, and then to the world. They have joined the human race. They fit in anywhere, no matter whom they are with. And no matter what happens it will be OK, because they have become part of the whole. There is a lot of peace in simply knowing you have a place, and a purpose, in the world.

Speaking of purpose, the next promise is about just that.

No matter how far down the scale we have gone, we will see how our experience can benefit others.

It's difficult to talk about a situation with someone—even a doctor or therapist—who doesn't have a clue as to what you're talking about because she hasn't lived through a similar experience. That's because you're not talking about the actual situations but rather the feelings associated with the situations. Putting your feelings into words can be a challenge; trying to convey them to another who doesn't have a clue, nothing more than an exercise in frustration. I remember a young woman who was residing in a long-term treatment center for several addictions. She said to me, "They gave me a new counselor. Not only is she not an addict, she's a virgin. How in the world am I supposed to talk to her?" She made a good point.

A 12-step meeting is one of the few places where the people whose stories are the worst, whose climb out was the hardest, are the ones most frequently sought out. Why? The understanding is there without the need of a lot of words. You know they know because they've already traveled the path you're on. There is nothing worse than well-meaning people who use platitudes like "I know how you feel" and "I can imagine how you feel" when you know perfectly well they don't have the slightest idea of what you're going through. I experienced a lot of this when my children died.

I felt like screaming, "How do you know? Have you buried your children?" I knew they couldn't possibly imagine the enormous pain that literally took my breath away at times, that lived in me every moment, that I thought would surely kill me.

In a 12-step program, when we encounter a problem of which we have no personal experience, we are encouraged to admit that and guide the person to someone who has had a similar experience. There are enough people in the meetings that a person who listens carefully to the stories of others will be able to find someone who truly understands. It's said that if you sit around the meetings long enough, you will hear your story.

In time, others will hear your story and seek you out because they know you will understand. By sharing your experiences and how you came out on the other side of them, what you learned about yourself, and how you dealt with the feelings, you will give them hope. When you see the light of hope in their eyes and know that in some small way you have been instrumental in putting it there, all those seemingly awful things that happened in your life will be put in perspective. You will realize that those very things have become a wonderful tool that you can use to help those who are still suffering.

That feeling of uselessness and self-pity
will disappear.

The irony of addiction is that the very things that addicts seek—a need to belong, a sense of well-being, a feeling of purpose—are exactly the things they must give up while practicing their addictions. To maintain a self-destructive lifestyle, addicts need to tell themselves their behavior is justified; this is commonly known around 12-step meetings as the "poor me" or "why me?" syndrome.

One of the wonderful things about attending meetings and hearing the stories of others is that eventually addicts will learn to ask, "Why not me?" They will come to understand that no one is exempt from troubles and pain and that the circumstances of their lives are not as important as what they did with them. Life can be a great place of learning for those who pay attention.

Another thing that takes place is that addicts begin to relate to and care for others, even to the point of wanting to help. There is no quicker way to get out of self-pity than to help another suffering human being. That can be the catalyst for finding a feeling of purpose. Through helping another, addicts help themselves.

Little by little, as addicts remain in recovery, attend meetings, and work the steps, they will give up the role of victim and move into the role of mentor. Self-esteem and self-respect will rise, a reason to get out of bed in the morning will move them forward, and those feelings of self-pity and uselessness will slip away.

People want to know that if they dropped off the face of the earth, someone would care. They want to feel as if they have left some small mark on the world, something that made it a little better place. A 12-step program gives people that opportunity. It began with two drunks helping each other, and the ripple effect has been amazing. Lives have been changed—not a little, but drastically—and those changed lives have touched many other lives. There may not be any front-page headlines or television stories, but lives have been saved, and the world is a better place for it. How can anyone be part of something so enormous, so wonderful, and continue to feel useless or stay filled with self-pity?

We will lose interest in selfish things and gain interest in our fellows.

Twelve-step meetings are made up of people of every race, gender, socioeconomic class, and occupation. Because it is an anonymous program, only first names are used. In that situation, everyone is on the same level. It's John, Mary, Ted, Cindy, and Jack—not Doctor So-and-so, Judge So-and-so, or convict so-and-so. It's simply people who suffer from addictions, who are searching for a better way to live, addiction free.

Although it may seem strange to an outsider, it's not uncommon to see a person who has spent years in prison and done horrible things mentor a priest, or to see a high school dropout helping a teacher. Addiction isn't about intellect, money, status, or what type of work a person does. It's about one addict who understands, who has traveled that well worn 12-step path, sharing his experience, strength, and hope with another.

Those who have been down that road, who know what it means to be a part of a 12-step program, who haven't forgotten where they started and why, will drop everything—no matter what is going on in their own lives—to help, or to find help, when the call comes. They know that how they behave in that one moment when the still-suffering addict calls for help could be a matter of life and death.

They answer the call without judgment or expectations, and they carry the message of their own recovery. There are no sermons, shaming, or guilt games, but rather a sharing of where they've been, what worked for them, and where they are now. They plant the seed of hope knowing that it grows in God's time.

It's not always convenient or easy, and it is seldom enjoyable, to give time, energy, and caring to a puking drunk who wants to argue about everything; to clean up a drug addict who is still shaking and out of it; to watch a weeping ninety-pound anorexic whose body is breaking down before your eyes or a gambler in a frenzy because the money is gone, even the house payment, and she is afraid to return home.

You might think it a difficult moment for the addict in recovery who has plans for the evening, perhaps has paid money for tickets to a fabulous show months ago, when the call comes. It's not, though, because at one time that person was the addict at the other end of the line begging for help. What would he have done if no one had cared, if no one came?

Part of a 12-step program is to let the hand "always" be there, not just when you have nothing better to do. That's what it means to put away selfish things and care more about your fellows than you do about yourself. You will begin to see each call as an opportunity to give back that which was given so freely to you, and you will go with joy in your heart, with sincere caring, and with no hesitation.

No matter what one's accomplishments in life—money, fame, even awards—there is no higher calling, nothing more important, than being of service, making a difference in someone's life other than your own. That is truly the gift that keeps on giving.

Self-seeking will slip away.

Take note that in the Twelve Steps, the first word of the first step is *We,* and it is carried throughout. Feelings of isolation and aloneness are the fuel that feeds addiction. As long as addicts can convince themselves that no one cares, no one understands, no one loves them—that it is them against the world—the addictions are justified. However, when they do make it into recovery and come to understand the steps, that particular excuse is eliminated. They have become a part of the "we."

It will become clear to them, in a very short time, that they have always been a part of the "we" and that their addictions have affected those people around them, even society as a whole. Addicts take up the time, space, energy, and finances of doctors and hospitals; they can be a danger to total strangers, hurting others; and they tie up the courts and jails. They may tell themselves they are hurting no one but themselves, but that's not true. Addiction has far-reaching effects.

In their self-seeking they are like a child who wants what he wants, when he wants it, the way he wants it—who never considers the fallout and doesn't take responsibility for the consequences.

Through recovery in a 12-step program, that attitude is no longer an option. The three Rs are recovery, respect, and responsibility. Addicts begin recovery by eliminating the addiction. When they can do that and actually work the steps, self-respect is restored, and they can no longer do those self-destructive things that hurt not only them but others. When they respect themselves and live accordingly, they learn to give the same respect to others, to the world around them, because they have become a part of the whole.

Responsibility is about choices. Addicts in recovery know they have a choice in every situation. They also know that with those choices comes responsibility for how their choices affect themselves and others. They are not an island apart from the rest of the world. For every action there is a reaction.

After a time of living in recovery and thinking differently, respect and responsibility become habits, and addicts find themselves making choices with no agenda except to do the next right thing as they know it . . . for themselves and for others. Self-seeking simply slips away.

Our whole attitude and outlook on life
will change.

Imagine what it's like to dread every new sunrise, to believe that life is something to be tolerated. In the final stages of addiction, that is how addicts feel. That attitude can be turned around through recovery. Life will become something to be embraced, to look forward to on a daily basis. Addicts in recovery will discover that their best day in addiction was not as good as their worst day in recovery.

Through working the first nine steps, addicts have healed their wounds, discarded their baggage, and revealed their secrets. They can finally remove the mask, breathe fresh air, step off the stage, and be exactly who they are. In 12-step meetings, they have a perfect testing ground for showing the world the truth of who they are. It's a safe, nonjudgmental place where everyone is seeking the same thing. The specifics of the situations may be different, but the sentiments are the same.

The most commonly reported feelings are fear of never being good enough, confusion about how to fit in to the world, and anger over not being able to understand why what is happening is happening. Addictions allow addicts to slip on the mask of indifference, well known in 12-step meetings as the "I don't give a damn" attitude. However, deep within they do care; otherwise they wouldn't turn to addiction to face the world. Living in constant conflict between who they really are and the persona they present to the world makes for very unhappy human beings, which can lead back to addiction. It becomes a vicious cycle.

There is absolutely no way to work the steps without revealing the truth. Only the first step speaks of the addiction. The remaining eleven steps teach addicts how to live a life in recovery with a new attitude and outlook. I've heard the process compared to coming back from a near-death experience. There is clarity, colors are more brilliant and flowers more aromatic, and those things that went previously unnoticed or were taken for granted gain great importance.

There is nothing like nearly losing your life to instill gratitude for the simplest things. After all my years in recovery, I still thank the God of my understanding each night as I slip between clean sheets, with a full belly, for all that I've received. Most addicts stumble through life with blinders on, oblivious to their surroundings and others in their lives. In recovery, it's as if a light has suddenly been shined on the world: gratitude will always trump attitude.

Ella Wheeler Wilcox wrote, "Laugh, and the world laughs with you; / Weep, and you weep alone." She may have meant that a person with a poor attitude and outlook on life becomes tiresome even for those who care deeply for him. Eventually, addicts who already suffer from loneliness may truly find themselves alone. Paranoia, blaming others and life, self-pity, and anger are not conducive to healthy relationships. The sad part is that for addicts to maintain their addictions, they must hold on to those coping mechanisms to excuse their addictive behavior.

When an addict works the steps in recovery, every excuse for self-destructive behavior is eliminated. Addicts learn to live in the moment and appreciate that they always have a choice. Unburdened by the past and free of fear of the future, they can focus on the day at hand and on doing the best they can in whatever situation arises. If they do make a poor choice, the steps tell them there is a way to resolve the situation. Perhaps for the first time in their lives, they have guidelines and directions, if they choose to use them. They feel a lot of relief in knowing they have to deal with only one thing at a time, one day at a time, that their best has nothing to do with anyone else's best—that it's OK for them to be happy no matter what is happening outside of them.

The laughter comes, and it comes from deep within—a place of true happiness. They may find themselves smiling for no reason at all, when no one is around. When that happens, others will be drawn to them, wanting to spend time in their presence because they are a joy to be around.

The great burden of attempting to change the world and others will be released in knowing all they have to do is change themselves, their attitude, and their outlook on life. The secret of how to do that is revealed little by little as each step is worked. It's said that before they are halfway through the steps, this phenomenon will take place.

Fear of people and economic insecurity will leave us.

Many addicts suffer from a syndrome called *terminal uniqueness,* but this is simply another excuse to avoid giving up their addictions. When given solutions, they tend to play the "yes but" game. No matter the specific reasons, they are saying, "Yes, but I'm different, special, and my situation is unique."

In meetings, addicts will discover two things: first, that no human being is exempt from pain and problems; and second, that addictions are a temporary escape that will not outlast the pain and problems. Most human problems involve other people, and because addicts already have trust and intimacy issues, it's easy for them to transfer blame onto those people. "They," whoever they happen to be, are the reason, the problem. If "they" would change their behavior, the addict would not have to indulge in addiction.

For addicts who continue in their addictions, sooner or later "they" will all be gone, but the addiction remains. The longer it continues, the more vast the barrier between addicts and others, and the bigger the fear of others becomes. They convince themselves that no one understands.

Suddenly, in 12-step meetings, they are faced with rooms full of people who understand, who share their stories, and who know what it's like to have real relationships. In time, addicts in recovery will begin to see the similarities instead of the differences. That old foe *uniqueness* will slip away. The fact that it's not the job of others to make their lives better, that it's their own job and that it is a full-time job, will become apparent. What others did or didn't do loses importance as they discover that what was important was how they reacted and the choices they made.

It's easier to trust another person who is in the same boat. It's easier to get close to someone who understands addiction and the struggle for recovery. It's easier for addicts to lose the fear of others when they accept responsibility for their own lives. Once addicts are in recovery, the truth is that no one and nothing can make them return to addiction except themselves. When that truth is brought home, the barriers begin to crumble, and they realize they were not victims but volunteers.

Money, in and of itself, is nothing more than pieces of metal and paper that can be traded for goods and services. It is the perception of money that causes many addicts problems. Since addicts continually look outside themselves to fill the holes that live within, there will never be enough, whether it's love or money.

There are extremely wealthy addicts, dirt-poor addicts, and everything in between. Poor addicts might believe that if they had more money and possessions, they wouldn't have to escape into addictions. Well, if that were true, there wouldn't be any wealthy addicts. Economic insecurity isn't about the lack of money and possessions. It's about the importance people put on those things.

If a person believes her life will be fulfilled by money, possessions, and power, she will spend her life frustrated and disappointed, continually working toward the next temporary high, just like any other addict. Those types of highs are like a monster that lives within, one that has to be constantly fed but is never satisfied.

Problems left unattended become bigger problems, whether personal or financial. Through the Twelve Steps and a God of their understanding, addicts will realize there is a solution to every problem. They will learn the difference between an easy, temporary solution and a solution that will resolve the problem once and for all. The solution will not always be simple. In fact, because the problems have been avoided for so long, the solution will probably be that much more difficult and will take time.

The great thing about finding a God of one's understanding is that fear is replaced by faith. The stronger that faith becomes, the stronger one's faith in oneself becomes. This faith is what helps put all things into perspective. Addicts are no longer floating around out there with no purpose, no direction, no idea what to do with life, alone and afraid. They have begun to live in the solutions instead of the problems.

While working toward resolving relationship and financial problems from the past, addicts in recovery will be living in a way that keeps them from compounding the problems with new problems. With time, the past will be put to rest and their lives will not be filled with new problems they must face. By practicing handling problems that once seemed insurmountable, living one day at a time, taking care of business when it arises, and holding tight to their faith that everything will work out for the best in the long run, they will lose their fear of people and economic insecurity. They can live comfortably in the skin they were given, understanding that relationships with others aren't about compromise and conflict but about love, acceptance, and living in the truth of who they are.

You can pray for anything, even for help with financial problems. The answer might be a second job at which you barely earn enough to pay off an old debt, or the need to sell a precious item, but a solution will be put in front of you. Sometimes, it seems to me, the more a person has to give up, the more he gets out of the act of giving things up. When you have taken responsibility, done whatever needed to be done, and taken care of business in an honest way, the feeling you take away is more valuable than any piece of green paper or possession.

You cannot put a price on self-respect and self-esteem. With each achievement in those arenas, you will discover that no matter what happens, where you are, or what you are doing, there will always be enough. Your God will not give you a free ride but will always help you find your way; and even if it's not the easier path, it will be the best path. That is when you will know for certain that faith and fear cannot abide in the same space.

We will intuitively know how to handle situations that used to baffle us.

When an addict is active in addictions, her instincts will most certainly fail her. Time after time, her intuition—that quick and ready insight that is used to make rational decisions—is lacking because she cannot see clearly. The addiction drops a filter in front of her eyes, one that changes her perception of everything.

Nonaddicts are amazed at what addicts are willing to give up to feed their addictions. One of the things they give up is the ability to make a rational choice without considering the addiction. When you live your life around the addiction, unable to truly trust your instincts, you will know what it means to be baffled by the simplest things—

decisions that nonaddicts take for granted. Going on a trip, out to a restaurant, out with other people, out to family gatherings—all these can become very complicated. Let's say that tobacco is your addiction. Laws now prohibit smoking in public places. You must be twenty feet from a main entrance to light up. This means you must consider how long you can go without a cigarette, what the weather is like outdoors, whether you can get away from the people you are with, whether you should drive or fly, whether you can be on an airplane that long—and on and on it goes. With all those things to consider every day, it's no wonder you're baffled.

If going to a restaurant or on an outing is that big a deal, imagine how overwhelming your other life choices can be when your addiction always takes the forefront. If you don't think your intuition is skewed through this thinking process, you are kidding yourself. That's what the second half of step 1 means: "our lives had become unmanageable." It's impossible to manage your life in a healthy way while trying to constantly manage your addiction.

Addictions can lead you to places you don't want to be, with people you don't like, doing things you don't want to do. You may be appalled at your behavior but nevertheless find yourself repeating the same scenarios over and over. In recovery, as you look back, you may become convinced you can't trust your instincts . . . that you can't trust yourself.

Through working the steps, and given time, practice, and faith, you will be able to trust your instincts. Living in an unaltered mental state or removing unhealthy compulsive behavior will elicit certain things. You will begin to consider the consequences of your actions—not only for yourself, but for others. You will know that what you do today will become your past tomorrow. Accepting life on life's terms, and understanding that if you make a poor choice there is a remedy and that you are never truly alone—these will be the beginning of the self-trust that will lead to an ability to trust your instincts.

Skippe H. said, "There comes a time when you must put aside those feelings of fear and doubt, and just do the next right thing." In the deepest, most honest place, addicts know the truth. They know what the right thing to do is. The right thing is seldom the easiest thing. At first, it will be difficult to break those old patterns, but with practice it will become second nature. Every time they walk through the fear and overcome doubts, they make it easier for themselves the next time, and slowly they learn to trust their instincts.

It's easy to think of a homeless drunk pushing around a shopping cart filled with his possessions as one who is baffled by life. However, still-functioning addicts—no matter their addiction, no matter whether they still have family and friends, a job, a car, and maybe a house and money in the bank—can, and many times do, suffer from the same problem. Remember, addiction is not about status, money, jobs, or anything else outside the addict. It is an inside job. The agony that lives within doesn't necessarily show itself on the outside. It's those feelings of being on the outside looking in, of not fitting in with other human beings, of having no real sense of purpose, that keep addicts baffled.

One important thing addicts learn in a 12-step program is to stop comparing their insides with everyone else's outsides. When in that mind-set, they will always come up short and be left feeling confused and bewildered about why they can't be what the rest of the world "seems" to be. Imagine what the world, and others, would look like if the truth of their wounds showed on the outside. That's exactly what happens in a 12-step meeting. Those in sincere recovery put it all out there: what it was like while living in the addiction, what happened to get them into recovery, and what it's like now. Their openness allows other addicts to see that they are not stupid, incompetent, or bad, but that they suffered from addiction. Knowing what happened to others lets them know that there is a turning point. Knowing what it's like now for others gives them hope.

The steps, together with help from others in recovery, will give addicts a new day and a new way—not just to live, but to think. Working the steps is a process of learning to act rather than react to situations, people, and feelings. One little saying that is posted on the walls of many a meeting place is this: "Think, think, think." It may seem simple enough, but for addicts in recovery, the idea of attempting to change the way they think is profound. It means taking a step back, considering all the options and ramifications for all involved, and asking whether the choice is something they can live with for a day, a week, a month, a year, or ten years down the road. The object of living in recovery and working the steps is to stop doing those destructive things that inevitably lead the addict back to the addiction. Figuring out that the addict has a choice in absolutely everything he does, and that he is responsible for those choices, is a big step away from being baffled.

There is no conflict in a mind that has found a road map through life. The directions are clearly stated in the steps, and if those directions are followed, the steps will lead addicts out of the darkness into the light. There will always be life problems, painful relationships, loss, health issues, and hardships, but those in recovery know that for every problem there is a solution—that, as my friend Destiny says, "If I just do the next right thing, everything will be OK."

If I am practicing my third step, turning my will and life over to the God of my understanding each day, God will speak to me through my instincts. Because I believe that, I can now trust my instincts, put my questioning and agendas aside, and know that if I do the next right thing as I understand it, the results are out of my hands.

We will suddenly realize that God is doing for us what we could not do for ourselves.

A 12-step program is not religious, but it is based in spirituality. There are members that represent every religion, as well as agnostics and atheists; therefore, religion is not a topic for discussion. Addicts are encouraged to find a Higher Power, or a God of their understanding, as part of their program. Some simply use their group as a Higher Power in the beginning. It's said that as a result of working the steps, addicts will have a spiritual awakening. This is when many addicts find a God of their understanding: during the process.

Spiritual awakenings are varied and diverse; they happen in whatever particular way people say they do. A spiritual awakening is that moment when addicts truly feel the connection to something larger than themselves. It is a profound moment. Suddenly, addicts understand they are no longer alone and never have to be again. There is a feeling of peace and purpose. They realize that all the occurrences, good and bad, in their lives are what brought them to that moment. They have come home.

It is through this spiritual awakening that addicts' lives are forever changed. Suddenly, they realize that this God of their understanding is doing for them what they were never able to do for themselves. Addicts who have been dependent on their addictions for so long are amazed to find themselves able to believe, for the first time, that they have a choice, and that they never have to return to those addictions again. Many would tell you that this could not have happened without divine intervention. Even before they asked for help, a God of which they had no understanding was looking out for them. That God put in their path the opportunity for them to find recovery. This is evident in the stories shared in meetings. The addicts end up in a strange place; a person they've never met crosses their path, or a sign or advertisement keeps showing up in front of them; then, they recognize that the person or message is for them. Is it coincidence? They don't think so.

I recall the story of an addicted woman who went through years of psychotherapy after being institutionalized for problems directly related to her addictions, and who believed she was cured. Later, she agreed to speak with a group of professionals about addiction. She, together with a doctor, a policeman, a minister, and a paramedic, spoke at schools, churches, and hospitals. Like the others, she shared her story, from a cured addict's point of view. Unlike the others, when she returned home after the meeting was over, she indulged in her addictions.

Before one talk, a friend told her that a person from a 12-step group was interested in hearing her story and would be at the next gathering. He came. She spoke. Afterward, he approached, told her how much he enjoyed her talk, and then handed her a slip of paper with his name and phone number written on it. He said, "Just in case you ever need us."

Enraged, the woman glared at the paper, and as soon as he walked away, she crushed it and tossed it into the nearest trash can. Less than two months later, brought low by her addictions and sitting in the middle of the floor rocking back and forth, filled with a tangible fear that she would be taken away to a mental hospital again, she flashed on the man's name. Desperate, she searched the phone book for him, praying he was listed. He was, she called, and he answered. It was the beginning of her recovery. Coincidence? She certainly doesn't believe that to be true. She believes he was sent by a merciful God, whom she came to know much later, to give her an opportunity, the chance for a life that she could never have imagined. Just as the man was an instrument in her life, she became an instrument in the lives of others, and they will become instruments through which God will work to help others find recovery and the way home to a God of their understanding.

Even though this woman had been addiction-free for a number of years and considered herself cured to such a degree that she could control her addictions when she returned to them, she had no support system, no steps to teach her how to live, and, most important, no God to give her guidance and hope. Those are the things she found in a 12-step program. Every day when she gets on her knees to turn her will and life over to the God of her understanding, she knows that no matter what occurs around her in life, there is absolutely nothing she and her God can't handle, and that whatever happens will always be for her best. She has learned to live from the soul—that the God of her understanding is doing for her what she spent many years, in many ways, trying to do for herself, only to fail time and again. I know this story to be absolutely true, because I am that woman.

A priest told me he had to come to a 12-step program to figure out that God was his Higher Power.

A psychiatrist who received his diploma while incarcerated in a mental hospital for addictions shared with me that through the Twelve Steps, by seeking a God of his understanding, he found clarity, compassion, and unconditional love of humanity—which led him to excel in his field. But more than that, he was effective—truly able to help others, to know that the part of himself that is touched by God is the part that tells him exactly what to do, the words to use, and how to act. There was no doubt in his mind that he was given a message and that it was a gift from God; he feels he has become a messenger of change and hope.

I met a woman of the streets—let's call her Susan—who had given up on others, life, and any notion that there was a Higher Power for her. She dug through trash cans and panhandled in order to survive. She would drink anything alcoholic to deal with her depression, anger, and resentments. While sitting on a bench in an upscale neighborhood, her bottle of whiskey well hidden in a fold of her filthy skirt, she waited for well-to-do passersby to hand her the guilt money she knew eased their conscience for having so much more than she had. She hated them, but she took their money.

Most people would walk by quickly, tossing some coins or a few dollars her way, and then scurry off; others simply looked away and walked faster. One afternoon, a well-heeled woman stopped and sat down on the bench next to her. As was Susan's habit, she held her hand out, hoping for money. The woman dug in her purse and came out with a pen and paper. She wrote something on it, handed it to Susan, smiled, and went on her way. When Susan unfolded the paper, she saw the woman's first name, her address, and the letters "AA" in bold black writing. She let out a cynical laugh and stuck the card in her bra.

When the weather turned cold and the shelters were full again, Susan searched out the slip of paper, which had found its way into an old handbag in her cart. She thought maybe she could get warm for a while and that the woman might give her something to eat, even some money.

Susan hesitated outside the nice house, its lights blazing in every room. It looked as if there was a party. A cold wind blew against her, chilling her to the bone, and she hurried up the stairs to knock on the door. The woman answered, smiled the same as before, and said, "You're just in time."

Susan stepped through the door into her first 12-step meeting. People hugged her, welcomed her, and brought her coffee and doughnuts. She recalls, "They didn't even seem to mind that I was dirty, smelled like a wet dog, and had open sores on my face. It was the first time in a long time anyone wanted to touch me on purpose." Curious, after the meeting she asked the woman why she had bothered with her. The woman said it was what God wanted her to do—that Susan was the woman's very special gift.

That spooked her. She thought she'd gotten into some kind of cult. As she was thinking about leaving, she realized it had begun to snow. The woman invited Susan to stay the night. Maybe just one night, Susan thought. She was surprised to learn that several women lived in the house, and all had suffered from one addiction or another. By the following morning, Susan had decided to stay. She said, "I don't know if it was the shower, the soft, warm bed, the other women, or what, but I didn't want to leave."

When she began to detox, the women stayed with her, bringing her back to health with love, compassion, and lots of prayers. They didn't tell Susan she had to believe in God or pray, but they did give her a book that contained the Twelve Steps. Unlike the shelters and churches she'd been accustomed to turning to in times of need, the women did not require her to do anything in order to be taken care of, fed, and clothed. She didn't even have to read the book, but it was hers to keep if she wanted it.

Still confused by the women's kindness to a stranger, that they had no expectations of her, Susan began to think— to wonder at the strange turn her life was taking. They'd accepted her into their household as if she'd always belonged there. Their three meetings a week were available to her, but she didn't have to attend. Sometimes she would sit on the staircase, where no one could see her, and listen. They talked a lot about this God of their understanding. Maybe, she thought, if it worked for them, it might work for her.

She went to her room, sunk to her knees at the side of the bed, and said, "God, if you're there, do you think you could help me?"

Even though she had no idea what was left for her in life, or even what she wanted out of life, Susan was given a life that would exceed what might have been her wildest imaginings. She told me she had no doubt that God had done for her what she could not do for herself.

Susan's is but one of many stories of real addicts whose lives were changed by turning their will and life over to a God of their understanding. As many people as there are in 12-step meetings, there are that many stories of how they found a recovery program, and a God. The one common thread I've heard is that not one of them believes it happened by accident, and that the one thing that brought about the most profound changes in their lives was opening themselves to a God of their understanding and allowing that God to do for them what they could not do for themselves.

Are these extravagant promises? We think not. They are being fulfilled among us—sometimes quickly, sometimes slowly. They will always materialize if we work for them.

The key words in the final promise are *always* and *work*.

Does a 12-step program "always" work? Yes. There are those who have tried the program, returned to their previous way of living, and said it didn't work. What didn't work, though, is the person. It's said that half measures will avail addicts nothing. There is no such thing as a little recovery, a modicum of honesty, a smidge of open-mindedness, or a wee bit of spirituality when you're working a 12-step program. To realize the promises is an all-or-nothing undertaking. The benefits of the Twelve Steps are in direct proportion to the amount of "work" you put into the steps.

Bob C. used to say to newcomers, "Wait for the miracle." He said that to me. I knew it would take a miracle, but I wasn't sure I wasn't a hopeless case. That is, until I began to truly listen to the stories of others whose lives had been as bad as mine, or worse. Even then I wasn't certain what the miracle was, but I wanted to find out if it could possibly happen for me.

Though I was so resistant to actually working the steps, I did two things right: I didn't indulge in my addictions; and I attended lots of meetings. I grabbed on to that first step for dear life. And I thought that between it and the support groups, it would be enough. It was for a while.

While attending the meetings, I watched others come in and get it. Meanwhile, I stayed stuck, hanging on by my fingernails, fighting the urge to return to my addictions on a daily basis. I will never forget a young man named Charley Bob. The first time I met him, I thought he was brain damaged. Although much younger than I, he looked old and was dressed in ragged clothing; he had on a pair of old moccasins that had seen better days, the toes turned up and stiff from being out in the weather. He'd lived through terrible abuse that lasted for years, and had found solace in addictions.

In a matter of a few months, this young man blossomed before my eyes. He went from being someone who was actually sleeping in a real doghouse, with no hope for the future, to being a clean, employed young man with a bounty of friends and the gift of being able to share his story openly and honestly, to help others. I wanted what he had, but I had not been willing to do what he did to get it. What was he doing that had eluded me? He was working the steps, whereas I was just sitting in meetings, believing I could coast through recovery without working at it, just as I'd thought I could coast through life.

I watched and listened to the miracle that was Charley Bob. He was doing those things that I talked about, that I pretended I was doing, and he was receiving those things that I desired. I don't mean a job, possessions, even friends. He'd found peace and serenity, a calmness of spirit, mind, and body, and I was still living in constant conflict. My conflict was rooted in my knowing what needed to be done, through the stories of Charley Bob and others like him, and not having the willingness to do it. I was like a carpenter with all the right tools but no desire to build.

Every tool I needed to construct a better life was laid out for me in the Twelve Steps. The solution was to pick up each one and use it to the best of my ability. Learning to use new tools is not easy, but with practice I got the hang of it. I stayed in the meetings, waiting for the miracle, but I also realized that waiting wasn't enough. I had to work for the miracle as well.

One by one, every promise was fulfilled in my life, and that—for anyone who knew what I'd been like, who knew the things that had happened to me and the things I'd done—is truly a miracle. Most who come into recovery in a 12-step program believe that the promises are extravagant if not impossible. Like me, even when they begin to do the work, they are still amazed when the promises come true.

The promise says, "They will always materialize if we work for them." The first nine steps will give us the tools to work toward the promises, and the final three steps will teach us how to hang on to them.

maintenance steps

Step 10

We continued to take personal inventory and when we were wrong promptly admitted it.

Step 10 is the first of three maintenance steps that allow recovering addicts to sustain the new way of life they have chosen. Some in recovery stop after step 9, not understanding the importance of the final three steps. They have done the work, are feeling better and attending meetings, but have no idea what is coming their way. Suddenly, they hit an emotional bottom or have a crisis of faith.

One thing I know for certain—from my personal experience and from the experiences of others—is that unless we can take our recovery out into the world each day, in all things, we will continue to live in conflict. Conflict is a mental struggle resulting from incompatible or opposing needs, drives, wishes, and external or internal demands.

A prime example of this scenario is the story of Tammi C. I'll never forget the moment when she first walked into a meeting I attended regularly. She was strikingly beautiful, although certainly world-weary. There was a lot of sadness, and anger, in her eyes. She shared that she'd been in and out of many detox units but was now in a long-term recovery program for women, and she believed herself to be ready this time to work the Twelve Steps.

Over the years I watched her struggle with each step, helped her when she would allow it, and was thrilled for her when her life began to level out. She got back her two children, whom she'd lost custody of years before owing to her addictions. She had a job and a decent place to live. I could see what was happening on the outside, but not on the inside. There, she was in conflict.

Tammy said, "At eight and a half years in recovery, I had reached a crisis point. My character defects reared their ugly heads and began to rule my life yet again. I'd studied the steps, worked them to the best of my ability, went to lots of meetings, spent time with others in recovery, but my addictions lingered on, even though I wasn't indulging in them at the time. The thing was that I continued to live, and think, the way I did while in the throes of my addictions.

"I'd just turned thirty, was in the middle of a divorce, and had started going back to my old haunts, running with others active in addictions. I began to neglect my children, lessened my contact with the meetings, and forgot about the steps and the God of my understanding. By the grace of God, I was confronted by others who cared deeply for me and about my behavior, and was told that my solution could be found in step 10."

I call this the "I have arrived" syndrome, and it tends to hit after step 9. In essence, those who fall into this syndrome are saying, "OK, I've done the steps. I'm not using, abusing, or acting out my addictions anymore. So I don't need any more of this 12-step stuff. I'm good to go." If it were only that simple. But it's not. Recovery in a 12-step program is a lifetime proposition.

Tammi returned to the meetings and said, "I'd always felt different, even in the meetings. I heard others speak of happiness and peace, of a relationship with their Higher Power and the gratitude they felt, but I'd only had fleeting moments of those things. In spite of my efforts to work the steps earlier, I realized I'd stopped after step 9, and I'd only done those in half measures. In that moment of clarity, I knew how sick my soul was: I was consumed by self-centeredness, fear, dishonesty, and resentments."

Step 10 isn't just about wronging others and admitting it; it's also about wronging yourself. What Tammi did was not affecting others in the 12-step program, but it was affecting her and those who counted on her. Tammi took an inventory, got honest, and admitted she was wrong in the way she'd been living and thinking. She said, "Facing step 10, coming to understand it, was the beginning of the life I enjoy today."

When she took her problem to the meetings, others shared their experiences with her. The first suggestion she heard was that she needed to stop running. She said, "I was always on the run, surrounding myself with other people. I couldn't stand to be alone, living in my own skin, my thoughts. It would be something I would have to force myself to do. But I had to do something to take me out of my misery. I started every day by telling myself God is in charge, even before I got out of bed. That helped me to focus on spirit-based living instead of self-directed living.

"The next thing was doing those things that needed to be done that day. It was about learning the very basic skills of living: setting a wake-up time, shower time, regular bedtime. I couldn't believe how childish and irresponsible I'd been. In practicing these simple changes, I was able to move toward the bigger issues my self-centeredness and fear were dominating. I'd failed my children, my relationships were unhealthy and harmful, and fear was keeping me from my potential. It was time to take a personal inventory each day to figure out who I was, what I was doing, and what I could do to fix it—and to do whatever it took promptly." Tammi was ready to end the conflict in her life.

I have been friends with Tammi for over twenty years, and I hope that we will be friends for a lifetime. I know how she lives her life. I know that she incorporates step 10 into her actions and outlook every day. She lives in the truth of who she is.

She said, "I'm not sure I do 'wrong' in the traditional sense. I don't lie, manipulate, or steal, and I haven't for a long time. However, what I've focused on for many years is admitting to and making amends for the harm of allowing the sickness in my soul to compromise my relationship to the God of my understanding and to the people in my life. Because at times I can wake up nasty for no reason at all and cause harm or say and do the wrong things, I must pay close attention to my defects and right my wrongs in the way I live my daily life. I'm not perfect. If I were, I wouldn't need step 10. But I strive every day to overcome that scared, mean, self-driven shell of who I was. Every day that I practice honesty, love, courage, strength, and forgiveness, I am righting the wrong of my addictions."

Like me and many others, Tammi hit an emotional bottom and had a crisis of faith while in recovery. We are recovering not simply from addictions, but from the life we lived around our addictions. The first nine steps will be the foundation for a new way of life, but step 10 will be the beginning of building the life that we so dearly desire.

By taking a daily inventory and taking care of whatever needs to be resolved promptly, I stop fears, anger, discontent, and conflict from getting a foothold in my life. Those are the very things that took me to addictions in the first place, and they could surely take me back there if I was unwilling to work step 10 every day. Even if I am able to stay in recovery from my addictions, I will still be unhappy, still living in conflict, if I cannot live in recovery of life each day.

If you are wondering what became of Tammi, I can tell you. She returned to school, earned a master's degree, got a job at a treatment facility for addictions, and is a good mother and, now, a doting grandmother. She says her successful life began when she encountered step 10 and began to implement it on a daily basis.

Step 10 says that we "continued" to take personal inventory and that when we were wrong, we promptly admitted it. That is exactly what it means. You'll notice it doesn't specify what is right or wrong or tell you that it's only about your actions or other people. A personal inventory is about you: your thoughts, feelings, and actions. How are you treating yourself? How is that affecting others? Are there things living in your mind and heart that keep you fearful and unhappy? What can you do to put them to rest? The time is now. Don't let those opportunities that can change your life for the better pass you by. The more promptly you handle a situation, the less chance there will be for it to take root and cause you problems.

When you are doing a daily inventory, you will recognize when a problem has cropped up because you will be able to see where selfishness, dishonesty, resentments, and fear have motivated your feelings, thoughts, and actions. The solution is simple, but it is not always easy. First, ask the God of your understanding to remove whatever stands in your way, and then take action quickly.

If it's so simple, you might ask, why is it so difficult? When things are going well, and we are happy and content, it becomes easy to get lazy, forget about working the steps, put off daily prayer, and slack off attending meetings—the very things that brought us to happiness and contentment. I've always known that I have to be extra vigilant when my life is at its best. Therefore, if when I take my daily inventory I see that I haven't done anything I need to correct, I turn to those things I have that I am grateful for, and where those things originated.

Randy B. said to me, "Don't ever forget what you were like, what happened, and what you are like today . . . and where you got it." Step 10, worked each day to the best of my ability, keeps that fresh in my mind, fills me with gratitude, and brings happiness and contentment, because I know that no matter what occurs in my life, there is always a solution. However, that works only when I am willing to incorporate the maintenance steps into my life every day. This may seem extreme, but your life could depend on it.

Step 11

We sought through prayer and meditation to improve our conscious contact with God as we understand God, praying only for knowledge of God's will for us and the power to carry that out.

Being a very human person, with all that entails, I find the prospect of writing about God daunting. I cannot presume to tell you what God looks like—whether God is a person, a spirit, or a mass of light; whether God is a he, a she, or something else. Does God live in the sky, in our hearts, or all around us? No human being knows these things. What I do know for certain is that my daily struggle—unhappiness, misery, and depression, along with my addictions—changed when I became willing to put my faith in a God of which I have no real understanding.

For those who have faith in a God, it's a very personal, unique experience. One thing I've discovered after years of sitting in 12-step meetings, working with others, listening to their stories, is that there is a difference between believing and knowing. Many believe there is a God, but their God lives in their minds. To *know* that there is a God is to feel that God lives in your heart and is reflected in the way you think, feel, and act on a daily basis. To me, a spiritual awakening occurs when a person moves from nonbelieving, or from simply believing, to knowing.

I've heard that for some in recovery, the spiritual awakening comes quickly and profoundly, but my experience has been that for most, it is a process. Step 3 teaches them to practice making contact with a God of their understanding, and step 11 suggests that they continually try to improve that contact through prayer and meditation. It's like saying to addicts, "OK, what you've been doing isn't working for you or you wouldn't be in your current situation. Why not give this God thing a try and see what happens. If it doesn't work, you can go back to what you were doing."

How do they know if this God thing is working? The truth will be revealed through changes. At first those changes may be subtle: a change of perception, realizing they see people and situations in a different way, noticing things that would normally escape them, having strange feelings of love and compassion creep in where there had once been anger and resentment, feeling a sense of belonging and of no longer being alone.

To improve anything, you must work at it, practicing faithfully and consistently, with an understanding that there is always more to learn, to experience, to strive toward. That's what step 11 is really about. You don't simply get on your knees one day, say to this God, "Here I am. Do with me what you will," and you're done. The book *Alcoholics Anonymous,* which is the foundation of all 12-step programs, says, "What we really have is a daily reprieve contingent on the maintenance of our spiritual condition."

As I'm writing about step 11, I'm thinking of myself and others who attempt daily to improve our spiritual condition. Susan T. comes to mind. For years, she had what most people would consider a glamorous job, working for an international hotel chain. Although she was making lots of money, meeting interesting people, and traveling worldwide, she continually suffered from severe depression, which resulted in one addiction after another.

Susan said, "I contacted a psychiatrist but lied to her about my addictions. After that, physically, mentally, and spiritually bankrupt, I walked away from my job, the money, and travel to return home to the Midwest, where I would find a way to heal myself."

Not only had Susan lied to the psychiatrist; she was lying to herself. She would continue holding fast to her addictions, in an out of relationships, jobs, and places she lived, for another ten years.

"After my father passed away and my best friend died of AIDS," Susan continued, "my addictions were the only thing I cared about. They were what numbed the unbearable pain of loss. After quitting another job before I was fired, I isolated myself in a basement apartment, venturing out only to feed my addictions."

If you had looked at Susan from the outside, you would have seen a beautiful, intelligent, confident woman working in an ideal situation; you could never have imagined what lived on her insides. And she was living proof that it's what lives on the insides that counts. No matter how much you have, how educated you are, or how well you can keep up a facade for the rest of the world, the truth of who you are abides within, and sooner or later it will see the light of day.

Susan found recovery in a 12-step program suited to her addictions, and continues to this day. She says, "What I learned about the steps is that there is a reason they are numbered the way they are. Step 1 had to be taken before I could take step 2, because I couldn't see a solution until I understood the problem. Step 2 gave me what I needed to make the decision to work step 3—turning my will and life over to the God of my understanding. To work step 3,

I had to get rid of all those things that were blocking me from God. That's what the action steps accomplish. Steps 4 through 10 put me into action and freed me from the wreckage of my past. I completed the first ten steps, and now I have carried out my decision in step 3 to turn my will and life over to the care of the God of my understanding. Only by practicing prayer and meditation each day will I receive God's will for me and the power to carry God's will out as stated in step 11.

"I believe that steps 3 and 11 are the foundation of my recovery. In step 3, I give up my self-will run riot. In step 11, I receive God's direction. It takes a lot of work—those action steps, and then practicing step 11 every day—but it is how I've learned to live from the soul, knowing that my insides match my outsides. Only my God knows the purpose I am here to fulfill, so I must come to rely on this infinite God rather than my finite self. When I do that it frees me from self-seeking motives, dishonesty, and self-pity. Aligning myself with God's will each day is the most important thing I can do to stay spiritually fit, which allows me to continue in recovery—not only from my addictions, but from the unhappy, depressed person I used to be."

I have been blessed to have watched Susan, and many others like her, turn their lives around through a 12-step program. We may come from different places in life, but we all ended up in the same sinking boat of addiction. The hand that pulled us up may look different to each of us, but we all describe it as our Higher Power, or a God of our understanding.

Once we are out of that sinking boat, step 11 will be our life preserver, keeping us afloat; it's the one thing that keeps us from slipping back beneath the surface. As long as we are afloat, there is hope that through prayer and meditation we will one day experience knowing our purpose here, and knowing that with God's help we will have the power and strength to carry out our purpose.

One of Susan's favorite prayers and mine, one that can also be used for meditation, is the eleventh-step prayer, the prayer of Saint Francis of Assisi:

> Lord, make me a channel of thy peace.
> Where there is hatred, let me sow love;
> where there is injury, pardon;
> where there is doubt, faith;
> where there is despair; hope;
> where there is darkness, light;
> and where there is sadness, joy.
> O Lord, grant that I may seek rather to
> comfort, than to be comforted;
> to understand, than to be understood;
> to love, than to be loved.
> For it is in giving that we receive,
> it is in forgiving that we are forgiven,
> and it is in self-forgetting that we find.

Susan says, "Some versions of this prayer end with 'It is in dying that we awaken to eternal life.' Self-forgetting is, in a way, a death. By learning to self-forget, my self-righteous and self-centered ego dies. Only then can I discover my true self and purpose in life: helping others. I ask, as Saint Francis did, for the grace to bring love, forgiveness, harmony, truth, faith, hope, light, and joy to every human being."

Beth, another woman in recovery, has a quote stuck to the wall in her meditation room: "Good morning, Beth. This is God. I am going to be taking care of everything today, so I won't be needing your help. Have a nice day." What a great reminder to stay out of God's business.

In working step 11 each day, I wake up knowing there is purpose for the day simply because I've been granted another day. I talk to the God of my understanding through prayer, praying "only" for God's will for me and the power to carry that out. I listen through meditation so that I might be able to make the best choices each day. For the remainder of the day, I pay attention to the truth of my thoughts, emotions, and actions. When I am practicing step 11, living in God's will for me, I know that whatever happens outside myself will not affect the happy, joyous, free person who lives within. Dwight S. told me, "You can't give away what you don't have." If I am to be of help to anyone else, I must first be spiritually fit myself.

Following are some prayers that you might use when considering step 11.

AN ADDICT'S PRAYER
Lord, we cannot escape each other;
You, because of your love for me,
I, because of my need for you.
Look at me often on the palm of your hand.
My special illness stems from a frightful Dependence.
Its recovery derives from a dependence on you
And on the Program.
Help me to lean on both. Amen.

THIRD-STEP PRAYER
God, I offer myself to Thee . . .
to build with me and do with
me as Thou wilt. Relieve me of
the bondage of self, that I may
better do Thy will. Take away
my difficulties, that victory
over them may be a witness
to those I would help
of Thy power, Thy love,
and Thy Way of life.
May I do Thy will always!

—*Alcoholics Anonymous,* p. 63

SEVENTH-STEP PRAYER
My Creator, I am now willing
that you should have all of me,
good and bad. I pray that you
now remove from me every single
defect of character which stands
in the way of my usefulness to
you and my fellows. Grant me
strength, as I go out from here,
to do your bidding.

—*Alcoholics Anonymous,* p. 76

SERENITY PRAYER
God, grant me the serenity to
accept the things I cannot change;
courage to change the things I can;
and the wisdom to know the difference.

PRAYER BY REINHOLD NIEBUHR
Living one day at a time; enjoying
one moment at a time. Accepting
hardship as the pathway to peace.
Taking, as He did, this sinful world
as it is, not as I would have it.
Trusting that He will make all
things right if I surrender to His Will;
that I may be reasonably happy
in this life, and supremely happy
with Him forever in the next.

There are no right words or wrong words, because any words spoken to God from your heart are what is needed. However, they are needed every single day. After all, if I told you that by giving up a little bit of time each day, by making some effort on your part, you could be cured of some horrible disease, wouldn't you be willing to do this? That's what I'm telling you, and step 11 is the solution.

Step 12

Having had a spiritual awakening as a result of these steps, we tried to carry this message to addicts, and to practice these principles in all our affairs.

Last night, as I sat in a local meeting, I heard a young man, Brad, who had been bused in from a long-term treatment facility, admit that he'd been in and out of many types of treatment but always returned to his addictions. He said, "I talked about the steps, said what was expected of me, but I never really worked them, and I have no spiritual connection."

It has been my habit to listen intently to those who have relapsed into their addictions, because I was told that I could learn from them what not to do. Over many years, listening to one story after another, I began to put together the common things that cause addicts to return to their addictions or to pick up new addictions. Like me, many other addicts have coasted through life conning others, not taking responsibility for their actions, and always finding someone to blame for their plight in life. I brought that person into recovery with me, believing I could do the same thing with the steps.

Even though addicts may be able to keep their addictions at bay, real recovery is about so much more. It's about healing the wounds—mental, emotional, and physical—that have been masked by the addictions. True healing comes through working the steps to the best of our ability, as completely and thoroughly as possible, and, as a "result," having a spiritual awakening. To awaken is to become fully conscious—"alert and aware," according to the dictionary. I find it ironic that to connect to the spiritual, addicts must actively embrace hard realities. The hard realities that must be faced are the following:

1. We have lost control.

2. We need help.

3. We have to "ask" for help.

4. What have we done?

5. How can we resolve or fix those things?

6. Whom have we hurt?

7. How can we resolve or fix relationships?

8. What keeps us from being the people we desire to be?

9. How can we rid ourselves of those things?

Recovery is about living in the truth, which for most addicts is a foreign concept. To function in addiction, addicts live in denial and delusion and act out through dishonesty, manipulation, and self-absorbed thinking and behavior. These things have been a way of life for them for so long that addicts can't imagine living any other way. But learn they must if they are to experience real recovery. What happens when addicts refuse to face those hard realities that are laid out in the first nine steps?

Let me introduce you to Doug D., who is a prime example of someone who was able to keep his addiction at bay for years but, when faced with a life crisis, realized that's all he'd done. I have known Doug, a big farmer in a small community, for over thirty years, both before and after he got into recovery from his addiction.

Doug was initially brought to recovery because after eight years of marriage and indulging his addiction, his wife left him. He said, "I figured it wouldn't hurt to get away for a while, have a little vacation. I packed my swim trunks, golf clubs, and racquetball racket and left for the treatment center." He was in for a big surprise, and whether or not he knew it at the time, had put his feet on a path that would forever change his life.

After treatment, Doug did all the right things. He attended lots of meetings, read the books, talked the talk, and thought it was all going quite well. His marriage was healing, and when he was nearly two years into recovery, his wife gave birth to a son. For thirteen years he remained in recovery and believed all was well. He said, "Things were good. I knew I hadn't worked the steps the way I should have, but I wasn't in my addiction, had gotten used to that, and life was OK."

Then, after fifteen years of recovery and twenty-three years of marriage, Doug realized something was wrong in his marriage. Suddenly, his life was totally unmanageable again. He said, "The pain was unbearable. I thought I would surely lose my mind. Fear gripped me."

Whether or not you are in recovery, life keeps happening. If you have not prepared yourself by working the Twelve Steps fully and completely, the way they are meant to be worked, you will be thrown back into those extreme emotions, that self-absorbed way of thinking that took you to addictions in the first place. What counts when real-life problems intrude is not how long you've been in recovery, but what you did with that time and with the steps.

Doug said, "I fell to my knees and begged God to help me, but as always, I never really felt that connection." Step 12 says that as a "result" of working the steps, we will have a spiritual awakening. In other words, if we work them—

really work them—it will happen. That hadn't happened for Doug yet—because the steps are suggestions; it's up to you how and when you work each step. However, believe me when I tell you that you get out of a 12-step program exactly what you are willing to put into it.

Twelve-step meetings are wonderful—a safe place for addicts to confide with others who understand. Talking to others who suffer the same addiction is therapeutic, because they know the truth of what it is to live in addictions. However, the meetings and the people are not the program. The program is set forth in the steps. You can listen to others, attend many meetings, and keep your addiction at bay, but until you actually work the Twelve Steps, you will never know the feeling of full recovery. It is one thing that no one else can do for you.

Doug never returned to his addiction, but he did return to the steps. This time, he did them in the order in which they were written, to the best of his ability. He didn't get his wife back, as she had moved on, but he did find recovery. He said, "Nineteen ninety-seven was the year I used to think of as the worst year of my life. Today, I understand it was one of the best years of my life. I had to work hard just to stay alive and not return to my addiction. I was forced to look at myself, and not once did I criticize my ex-wife. I began to see the promises come true in my life. I was told they would materialize if I worked for them. I did, and they did. Finally I could look into the mirror, into the eyes of others, and smile. I liked what I saw. I experienced every emotion there is since my real recovery, except one: shame. I haven't been ashamed of anything I've done since working the steps and having a spiritual awakening."

Steps 10, 11, and 12—a daily inventory, conscious contact with a God of our understanding, and working with others—are what keep us from becoming complacent in our program. I know from personal experience how serious a danger complacency can be. I had hit a really hard bottom, having lost pretty much everything and everyone in my life, when I came to a 12-step program. I was so grateful for a second chance, to have some help and direction to a new way of life. I worked hard at the steps, attended lots of meetings, and engaged with the people; life was good.

When I thought things couldn't get any better, they did. I was reunited with the love of my life, got married, moved to a fine house, and had more than I ever imagined in my life. I was truly happy for the first time. Maybe I didn't really need the meetings that much anymore. I had new friends and was running my own successful business. Did I have the time to give to others in recovery? Did I need to do an inventory each day? It wasn't like I was doing anything bad anymore. That's where my thoughts wandered, and they were closely followed by my actions.

As I slipped away from the meetings, from the people, and from working with others, my hard-won self-esteem became pure ego. I was told that when we are into ego, we "EGO" ("Edge God Out"), and that's exactly what I did. As

I pulled away from everything that had saved my life, believing that I was once again in control, it entered my mind that my addictions were again an option. When that thought came, I knew true terror. I returned to the meetings and the people, but most of all to the steps, those three maintenance steps that had allowed me to keep what I'd found, one day at a time. It is said around the meetings that when you get in a bad place and all else fails, help another who is still suffering. I came to know the truth of that statement.

The benefits of carrying the message to those still suffering from addiction are twofold. First, it reminds us of where we've been and reinforces the fear of returning. Second, it helps us to realize that all we went through is of benefit as long as it can help another, still-suffering addict, which in turn gives us a feeling of purpose.

How do we practice these principles in all our affairs? Doug D. said, "Today, I am a man who lives from the soul, and I'm true to myself. I am available to those who want what I have found. It's not my job to fix them, but to show them, through the way I live every day, that life can be wonderful, fulfilling, and fun." Having been fortunate enough to watch the changes in Doug, I can tell you that he carries the person he's become into every facet of his life.

Step 12 isn't simply about helping others in recovery, but about knowing that when we are spiritually fit, understanding that the God of our understanding puts us where we need to be, with the people we need to be with, each day, and we are given opportunities to help in a myriad of ways. We take the person we have become out into the world each day and live what we've learned. Someone once told me that it's not what we do in a 12-step meeting for one hour of our day but what we do with the other twenty-three hours that tells us who we are.

Every moment, every thought, feeling, and action, becomes important. When I stand in line at the grocery store behind an older person who is slowly counting out change to pay for her goods, how do I think, feel, and act? If someone cuts me off in traffic, what do I do? If I notice a distressed individual, addict or not, how do I react to that person? No matter the situation, big or small, what I do with it tells me who I am and if I am truly living what I believe. Instead of saying to myself, *I don't want to get involved,* I say to myself, *I am involved because I am a part of humanity.* That's when I know that the feeling of belonging has moved from a 12-step meeting to the world around me. I have become willing to put myself out there in a loving, compassionate, kind, nonjudgmental way, and if I do the next right thing, God will take care of the results.

The steps tell me to attempt to strive forward each day, no matter how imperfect I may feel. When I do make mistakes, and I will, there are ways to fix them, and if I do that promptly, I can avoid the great dramas that took me to addiction. The main thing I know is that ultimately I have choices in everything in my life, and I am responsible for *my* choices—not yours. Your choices are between you and the God of your understanding. I don't have to agree or disagree; I simply accept that if I'm entitled to mine, so are you. My purpose is to carry the message, not to attempt to carry the person down the path I think she should travel. Neva G. said to me, "If God needs any little helpers, he'll let you know. Otherwise, stay out of God's business."

What is the message? No matter where you've been or what you've done, there is hope, and every person who draws breath has value, and there is a purpose. I found my hope, value, and purpose through a 12-step program.

Conclusion

They are the people you encounter every day: bankers, trashmen, psychiatrists, teachers, city workers, doctors and lawyers, waiters and waitresses, priests and ministers, dog walkers, even movie stars and heads of state. Age, race, and social and financial status are not a factor. They come from every town and country. They are addicts.

Those who suffer from addictions are affected body, mind, and soul. Many have tried doctors with their vitamins and pills, psychiatrists and psychologists with their theories, even religion with its morals and values, to cure their addiction, only to fail time and again. What is it about a 12-step program that works when all else fails?

Twelve-steppers understand. Imagine what it would be like to have cancer and to explain it to someone who had never suffered from cancer—the anger, the fear, the feelings of helplessness and hopelessness. Consider how much easier it would be to take off the hat covering a head made hairless from chemo treatments, and talk with another person who truly understands from personal experience. You could speak openly and candidly about the disease, not having to explain yourself and your feelings. The barriers would fall away. You could laugh together, cry together, and know you were not alone in your disease. So it is with members of a 12-step group. They are surviving together.

It all started with one drunk helping another, who then helped another—and on and on it went over the years until the 12-step program was put down in a book called *Alcoholics Anonymous*. The Twelve Steps are meant to be a guide for those who want to live a better life. They are not rules. The people who wrote them were simply saying that this is what worked for them. If you want what they found, try these steps. However, please keep in mind that, as is made clear in the book, what you do, or don't do, is always a personal choice.

What you get out of a 12-step program, no matter your addiction, is directly related to what you are willing to put into it. Step 1 is the only step that mentions your addiction. Steps 2 through 12 teach a new way to think, to live, to relate to others and the world. By utilizing the simple wisdom of the steps in daily life, you can put the past to rest, restore your self-respect and self-esteem, and in recovery find some peace and happiness.

A 12-step program is not a religious program, but it is based in spirituality. What's the difference? Twelve-step meetings embrace people of every faith, people who have no faith, and people who are searching for faith. The program does not tell people what to believe, but it encourages them to seek out a Higher Power of their understanding. It is based on the belief that each individual has the right to choose, without censure or explanation, what she believes.

Addicts in recovery in a 12-step program live one day at a time, giving each day the best they can, with the knowledge that they cannot change the past and have no control over the future. They attend meetings to share their experience, strength, and hope with others, and to maintain their recovery. They are no longer alone, fighting their addiction and the world. They have been given tools, and they know that help is only a phone call away.

One life touches another, which touches another, until millions of otherwise helpless, hopeless addicts find a better way to live. Through this ripple effect, these addicts in recovery become better people, parents, spouses, workers, spiritual leaders, doctors, therapists, and so forth. The ripples get wider and broader, touching many lives in a positive way.

Through working the Twelve Steps, addicts learn about keeping life in perspective. They come to understand that it's not about money, possessions—even accomplishments—but about who they are every moment of every day, and how they treat others and themselves. For them, life becomes a gift on a daily basis, never to be taken for granted. For many, it is not a second chance at life, but the first chance they have ever had to know what it is the program promises. If they are rigorous, honest, and willing to work the steps, they will be happy, joyous, and free.

The dictionary says that a miracle is a wonder, a marvel, an extremely outstanding or unusual event. In a 12-step program, it is a common occurrence. For instance, I once heard John T. share his story. He was a homeless wino when he walked into a meeting three decades ago. He said, "Wine sores covered my face and body, I wore ragged, dirty clothes, and my body odor offended even me. I had been treated like a leper in hospitals and shelters, had been spoken to as one would talk to an ignorant child. I knew that if I dropped off the face of the earth, no one would notice. A 12-step meeting was my last resort."

John walked into a 12-step meeting in a church basement on a Saturday night with the idea that if something didn't change, he would take his life. He said, "A man greeted me at the door with a warm handshake and a welcoming smile. A well-dressed woman approached. I knew she was coming to tell me to leave—but she hugged me. No one had willingly touched me, let alone hugged me, in years."

If you met John today, you would never imagine he was the man who walked into the meeting that Saturday night. However, you would know him, because he is always the first one up to greet the newcomer with a warm handshake, a hug, and a sincere welcome. He always says, "Welcome home." Since getting into recovery, he has been instrumental in helping others discover the miracle. The miracle is in the healing of the otherwise broken and discarded souls, many of whom would have given up on life if not for people like

John, who carry the message not only in their words, but in the way they live their lives every day.

Sandy P., a food addict who had lived an isolated life for years, with food her only companion, until she was hospitalized and nearly died, told me, "I couldn't stop eating. I wanted to stop eating. I tried everything, but nothing worked. I stopped going out because I couldn't stand the stares, and that I made others uncomfortable . . . even my own family. The more they came down on me about my weight, the bigger I got." The doctors told her she wasn't healthy enough to have the surgery to help her lose weight. The day Sandy was released from the hospital, knowing she would return to her life and her addiction, the woman who pushed the hospital magazine cart around handed her a note about an OA meeting the following night. For her, as for John T., it was the last resort. She attended.

I lost track of Sandy because I moved away. A few years later, as I walked through a mall in my hometown, a woman came up to me and hugged me. I had no idea who she was. It was Sandy. I asked her if she had had the surgery, and she said, "No, I got into OA." She twirled around, a look of pure joy on her face, and said, "What do you think?" She looked amazing . . . and happy. Over coffee, she shared with me the miracle that was her life.

Like me, John T., and Sandy P., countless miracles are out there walking around, alive, happy, and helping others through 12-step programs. Many of us would have died as a result of our addictions and of the way we lived had it not been for the Twelve Steps, the people, and a belief in a Higher Power. And if we had died, all the lives we have touched in a positive way might have gone by the wayside, too.

It's said that for everything we get, we must give something up. We give up time and energy for jobs and money. We give up money for those things we desire. So, what do we give up for recovery in a 12-step program? I gave up my addictions for freedom. I gave up my loneliness for those who understand. I gave up my fear for the belief in a God of my understanding. I gave up my role as a victim of life for choices. I gave up blaming others for becoming responsible. I gave up a life of misery for happiness and peace. What a deal!

People say to me that they can't believe all I've overcome and where I am today. I say to them, "I had a lot of help, for which I will be eternally grateful." The three things that brought me to a life beyond my wildest dreams are: (1) others who understand; (2) the Twelve Steps, which give me direction and purpose; and (3) a God of my understanding who loves me totally and completely even when I am very human. If you told me I could go back and never suffer from an addiction or have to work my way through recovery, I would have to say to you, "No, thank you." If you told me you would give me millions of dollars or valuable possessions to return to the life I knew before recovery, I would have to say, "No, thank you." This is truly one experience I wouldn't trade for anything. And I would do it all again if I had to.

When I think of all the people I've met that I would never have encountered in my life, the places I've been, the stories I've heard, the amazing experiences I've had, it's almost overwhelming. If you wonder why I stand in awe of my life on a daily basis, think of a young addicted woman who lost everything and everyone in her life, had no self-esteem or self-respect, had done horrible things, lived in fear and dread of each new day, and believed her life was cursed—and then grabbed on to the Twelve Steps that saved her life. Today, I could tell you about all the things I've acquired—my career as a writer, the many friends—but that's not what it's really about. It's about cherishing every minute of every day and knowing that each day is a new opportunity, each person I meet is worthy of my compassion and acceptance, and no matter what is happening around me, I am happy, joyous, and free. Only those who have been imprisoned through addiction know what it means to be free.

Conclusion

About the Author

Barb Rogers learned most of her life lessons through pain, tragedy, and addiction. After beginning her journey of recovery, Barb became a professional costume designer and author of three books about costuming. She's also written *Keep It Simple & Sane: Freeing Yourself from Addictive Thinking, Twenty-Five Words: How the Serenity Prayer Can Save Your Life,* and *Clutter No More.* Visit her online at *www.BarbRogers inspirations.com.*

Printed in the USA
CPSIA information can be obtained
at www.ICGtesting.com
JSHW082346140824
68134JS00020B/1909

9 781573 244220